Pagan Portals
Abnoba

Celtic Goddess of the Wilds

Pagan Portals
Abnoba

Celtic Goddess of the Wilds

Ryan McClain

MOON
BOOKS
Winchester, UK
Washington, USA

JOHN HUNT PUBLISHING

First published by Moon Books, 2022
Moon Books is an imprint of John Hunt Publishing Ltd., No. 3 East Street, Alresford
Hampshire SO24 9EE, UK
office@jhpbooks.net
www.johnhuntpublishing.com
www.moon-books.net

For distributor details and how to order please visit the 'Ordering' section on our website.

ISBN: 978 1 80341 024 1
978 1 80341 025 8 (ebook)
Library of Congress Control Number: 2021947877

A CIP catalogue record for this book is available from the British Library.

Design: Matthew Greenfield

UK: Printed and bound by CPI Group (UK) Ltd, Croydon, CR0 4YY
Printed in North America by CPI GPS partners

We operate a distinctive and ethical publishing philosophy in
all areas of our business, from our global network of authors to
production and worldwide distribution.

Contents

Acknowledgments

I wish to thank my husband who has dealt with my constant indecision and rewrites of this book. He stood by my side through it all, no matter how stressful I may have made things on myself. You are my husband, my love, and my best friend. I love you more.

I want to offer my supreme gratitude to my mother and father. Your support and well wishes over the years has at times been a life preserver when I needed it most. The two of you have always encouraged me to follow my dreams, and here I am. There is nothing I can say to adequately express my appreciation, so I simply say, thank you.

I would like to offer praise to the Gods, Goddesses, Great Spirits, and Ancestors that have guided me on this path. Each step on this journey has been unique and imparted some form of wisdom. In particular I dedicate this book to Abnoba as She inspired every word.

I would also like to extend a special thanks to a few influential people on this path: First, to Segomâros Widugeni for his extraordinary work in the Gaulish Polytheism movement. This book is possible due to his extensive efforts and leadership. Second, to Letonelos Tarvogenos for his extremely helpful work with the Gaulish language included in this book. I would not have been able to utilize the language without your help. Finally, to Mandy for influencing me on this path oh so long ago. Your guidance meant the world to me.

Preface

I felt that I should take this opportunity to introduce myself and discuss how I got to this point on my path. This way the reader can gain a better perspective of where I am coming from. This is my first book and because of this I feel it is imperative of me to offer a bit of background. I hope that this will give you a better understanding of how I began my relationship with the Gaulish Deuoi (Gods), and in particular Abnoba. It has been a long journey indeed.

Early Years

I grew up in a very secular household. We never attended church. I am still grateful for this fact despite the unquenchable thirst for religion that I would later develop. We had the 'average' American Christmas, Easter, Fourth of July, and Thanksgiving of which many may be familiar. My parents believe in *a* God, but they were never big on going to church.

My love of polytheism was there before I really knew what it was. I remember in an elementary school art class we had to choose something from a magazine and try to replicate it. I chose a picture of the Egyptian Goddess Bast. A few years later we studied Greek mythology and I was completely enamored by all of the gods. We were to pick one of them and write a report. I wound up doing three reports because I could not choose just one. At the time it was completely beyond my comprehension that they were real and believing in them as divine beings was okay. I just knew that I was pulled towards them.

The first church service I ever attended was actually a midnight mass that I was dragged to by a couple of Catholic friends in high school. It was a strange experience to say the least. However, I was quite drawn to the music, the ceremony and the history of it all. I knew then that I wanted religion in my life; I just needed to find the right path for myself.

The years during my teens were really the beginning of my spiritual journey. Growing up as a gay kid in a small Midwestern town, I had an aversion for many years to organized religion as a whole. In my experience they were against everything I knew to be true about myself. It was around this time that I even declared myself an atheist. However, atheism did not last long. In my heart I knew this was not how I really felt. I knew there was something bigger than myself.

I spent a great deal of time self-reflecting. I believed in spirits and I believed in many gods. I was lucky enough that my hometown bookstores did have a few books on Paganism. However, despite all of the things I believed in I was unsure of what to label myself. For some reason that felt important to me. I needed to find a spiritual home.

Adulthood

It was not until I had moved out on my own that the research really began. At this point I had my own computer and I was able to study things online that I could never find at local bookstores or the library. A whole new world was opening up for me. I read about every religious path that I came across, but it was polytheism that held a strong place in my heart. I was able to read about Celtic and Norse Mythology for essentially the first time in my life. I was awestruck when I discovered that there were indeed other people who loved the old deities as much as myself, and who followed that type of path. So many gods to familiarize myself with, and I would spend years doing just that.

In fact, I spent the next 10 to 15 years studying the ancient mythologies of several cultures. Most notably I was called to the various Celtic and Germanic pantheons. I seemed to be on an endless loop of bouncing from one tradition to the next. I even had brief connections to deities from ancient Egypt and Mesopotamia, but no matter how inspired the connections they would often fizzle out. So much so that I began to feel like something was inherently wrong with me. I just could not find the right path for myself.

Finally, I began exploring the world of Gaulish Polytheism. The ancient inhabitants of Gaul were the continental Celtic people primarily living in the area of modern-day France, southern Germany, Belgium, and Switzerland. Gaulish Polytheism is known by various names. Among them is Senobessus, meaning 'Old Custom' which was coined by Segomâros Widugeni. Another name that is picking up steam is Galatibessus, meaning 'Gaulish Custom'. While there is no surviving mythology among the Gauls, the Deuoi and the culture fascinated me. There was such a strong connection that seemed to call out to me. There are still many other elements and cultures that my practice will focus on from time to time, but Gaulish Polytheism was that spiritual home I had been searching for.

My journey to Abnoba was not immediate. Several Deuoi popped up along my path. Cernunnos came first followed by Artio, Camulos and in particular Damona. There were even a few others in between each of them. They each gifted me with knowledge and growth. They have all remained important parts of my life and I still periodically give offerings to them. Through it all I feel as though they were preparing me for the relationship that I now have with Abnoba. Regardless of what part they did play, they all welcomed me into their world. It felt as though my whole life the Deuoi had been awaiting my arrival.

Introduction

I have spent years honoring many deities with varying levels of devotion. I have learned many lessons through their tutelage. However, something was always lacking. I sought that spark of divine revelation that I had read about from others. When it did not come, I felt discouraged. Little did I know that I had been receiving subtle messages most of my life. That voice that told me to stop on a hike and just absorb the divinity that surrounded me. That glimpse of a doe and her fawn gently moseying through the meadow. The quiet whisper of a light breeze as it makes its way through the woods. The signs were there. I was just not ready to receive them quite yet.

It certainly took some time for me to realize that the relationship I longed for was with the great huntress, Abnoba. In fact, as an avid *non*-hunter I was greatly surprised, to say the least, that She wanted anything to do with me. Still, Abnoba has been a diligent teacher and guide in my life. This book is an attestation to those lessons. Through them, I discovered numerous other roles that She holds sway over. I hope that this book reveals some of these aspects to you. It has taken intense study, contemplation and prayer to reach the conclusions that I have come to.

Abnoba is a rare goddess in the sense that She is not the most commonly worshipped deity. Many have heard of Her Roman counterpart, Diana, or Her Greek parallel, Artemis. Among Her fellow Gaulish Deuoi; Cernunnos, Artio and Sirona certainly seem to have numerous followers. I felt that Abnoba wanted the chance to speak and have Her voice heard. She pushed me quite a bit as I often lack the confidence to put myself out there. She instilled in me the courage to push down the boundaries that were holding me back.

I consider myself a reconstructionist, at least to some degree. Being historically accurate is important to me. However, in writing this book I knew I was going to have to introduce the reader to personal observations. These experiences, or UPG (unverified personal gnosis), is frequently frowned upon to some degree in many circles. At the very least it is not commonly discussed. The fact is that the Gaulish Deuoi lack the mythology that various cultures have. It is required that we put in the personal effort of getting to know the gods and goddesses that we honor.

I would not have the ability to write a book on Abnoba had I no personal interpretations to share. While I have tried to make sure that as much as possible is based on historical knowledge, I had to venture out from that. I really had to dig into my experiences to present a fuller picture of Abnoba. I have always wanted to write a book, but I never found the right subject. As a devoted student of Abnoba, I finally found my voice. It is my hope that what I have learned will serve you well on your journey.

Chapter 1

Encountering Abnoba

"Muse, sing of Abnoba, mother of the forest, the pure one who delights in arrows, who was fostered with Grannos. She waters her horses from the Danube deep in reeds, and swiftly drives her all-golden chariot through the towns to tree-filled Black Forest where Grannos, god of the healing wells, sits waiting for far-shooting delighter in arrows. And so, hail to you, Abnoba, in my song and to all goddesses as well. Of you first I sing and with you I begin; now that I have begun with you, I will turn to another song." Homeric Hymn 9 to Artemis (Translation Evelyn-White. p. 435)

The number of Deuoi from Gaul is vast, numbering in the hundreds. Some of these deities were known by several tribes over large areas, while others are tied to one specific location. For instance, the goddess Abnoba is intimately connected to the Black Forest region of Germany. That said, Her 'range' has extended well beyond that in the modern day. As a guy living in the Midwest of the United States, I can attest to that. Here we will examine how Abnoba came into my life, and the roles that She has since shown to me.

First Encounters

As a kid my friends always wanted to play sports. This was never my preferred activity; in fact, I abhor sports. Occasionally I lucked out and they felt like doing my favorite pastime. This was when we would sneak off to the woods just beyond the cornfields. We would carve pathways through the field to covertly sneak off to the forests as we were not allowed to go that far from home. We would spend what felt like hours just wandering and exploring. Sometimes we even ventured down to the local creek and splashed around. At the time it seemed as though it was a grand wonderland full of unknown mysteries waiting to unfold. I still feel this excitement when exploring the woodlands as an adult. I now live next door to the house that I grew up in and I still look at those same woods every day. Today I realize that this grand forest is not nearly the size I thought it was in my youth. I still feel so fortunate that I had this opportunity growing up. So many of us are far removed from these wild places today.

The woods have always been such a mystical place for me. I could get lost in the sounds of birds calling, or hearing the trees blow in the wind. There is a peace that settles over me that I am unable to put into words. I feel that through my infatuation with the forests Abnoba has been trying to reach out to me since those early days with my friends. It is strange that we can have those moments and not fully grasp the complexity of what is happening. Now, a walk in the woods is never taken for granted. I know that it was Abnoba leading me through the forest back then, and now She seems to be leading me through life.

Receiving Messages

Since beginning my journey as a Gaulish Polytheist I have felt a pull towards several Deuoi. However, it started to become clear that one in particular was trying to reach out to me. Unfortunately, for the longest time I was not sure who it was. I have always been a vivid dreamer, but one night in particular has always haunted me. I rarely speak of it because it was such a personal encounter, but that dream will forever remain ingrained in my mind. Essentially, I was approached by a woman, that through prayer and meditation I came to realize was a goddess, and I was given information about the death of my grandmother that came to fruition. After this, I would often have dreams about many different goddesses. I would try to reach out to them thinking that they were the one who had guided me that night. While they seemed happy to guide me for a bit, I would learn over time that they were not the one who had reached out to me on that fateful night.

Finally, after several years had passed, I dreamt of a goddess that was befriending all the animals that She came upon. This time the goddess felt very familiar. When I woke up, I was shaken. I had seen this goddess years before warning me of impending death. She was too familiar not to recognize. This time She did have a bow and arrow with Her so I had something to go on when seeking Her out. At the very least, I now had a starting point to investigate. I had only been working with Gaulish Deuoi so I was quite confident that She was Gaulish as well. After a general search I decided that it was time to explore Abnoba. She was a goddess I was already quite familiar with, but had not reached out to due to Her assumed connections with the hunt. I did not understand how I was supposed to connect with Her. I am not a hunter in the least.

I wanted to learn the importance of hunting to the Gauls so I began researching the subject. Hunting was not necessarily just a sport, but a *"daily exercise of skill and courage"* (Green, 1992, p. 53). According to Miranda Green, hunted food animals were actually quite rare at Iron Age sites equaling only about five percent of all animal bones (1992). The Greek historian Arrian offered numerous insights into the hunting done by the Ancient Celts. Perhaps most important though is his remark that the ancient Celts never went hunting without getting the blessings of the gods. Green summarizes this stating that *"hunting itself was a form of ritual activity which needed both the permission and assistance from the divine powers"* (Green, 1992, p. 62). She also remarks that due to the association of hunting with sport or sustenance, hunter-deities could be associated with war or abundance. This all goes to show what a sacred rite hunting was to the Gauls. If a life was taken in the hunt, then an offering was given to the hunting deity, in our case Abnoba.

While I still cannot bring myself to hunt, this does give me the ability to respect the activity as it was seen by the Gauls. However, a much more important aspect of Her that I picked up on was as a goddess of animals. This affection for animals is really what allowed me to connect with Her in the manner that I have. She seemed to be a protector of the innocence that animals represent to me. So, while She is a huntress, Abnoba holds great respect for all wildlife. Realizing all of this I was finally able to get on board that it was Abnoba who was trying to reach out to me.

You may be asking yourself why a goddess of the hunt was warning me about an impending death, after all, I asked myself this very question. As I began exploring Abnoba and found Her link to Diana things started coming together. Diana was a goddess of the hunt, yes, but she was so much more. She was a goddess with several spheres of influence such as women, healing, and even crossroads. Crossroads were linked to death in the Greco-Roman world. Through Diana's Greek counterpart, Artemis, I also learned that she had a role in the death of women. The pieces started coming together for me. Abnoba is not merely the Gaulish Diana, but I do feel that there was a reason the Romans connected these two goddesses. Over the years I would have other dreams relating to death and again it has been Abnoba that warned me during those instances as well. This is a guise of which I have become quite accustomed to seeing Abnoba in.

Developing a Relationship

After making these connections my journey with Abnoba really began. I started to reflect on my life. So many pieces started to come together. This is who had been reaching out to me all along. It is from this connection that this book came about. Anytime that I had become interested in a deity I had a strong desire to learn everything I could about them. This book is a result of that very journey with Abnoba. The purpose of this book is to offer other wandering souls a blueprint of sorts to begin their adventure with Her, but it is also an act of devotion dedicated to Abnoba.

As I have already pointed out in the introduction, and will point out again, much of this book is personal experience, or UPG. We simply lack the resources in Gaulish Polytheism that many other traditions have. There are no Gaulish myths, no exploits of the gods. In fact, sometimes all that we have is an inscription with a name attested to just one time. We are lucky in the fact that several inscriptions have been discovered with the name Abnoba. However, aside from these inscriptions, and a single statue, that is all of the information that we have on Abnoba.

It is through deep prayer, meditation and dreams that I have gathered the information that I now have on Abnoba. I have tried, when possible, to include only information that can be backed up by archeology. Unfortunately, sometimes we must dig deeper. However, you must not take my word as the final one. If you decide to honor Abnoba in your life She may show you things that She has yet to show me. Our experiences may be quite different from one another. Reach out to Her, and see what She has to show you.

In the process of getting to know Abnoba I decided to explore other goddesses of the wild from various Indo-European peoples. I feel that, by taking a cue from the Romans, it is possible to understand the Gaulish Deuoi a little bit better through comparing and contrasting them with other Indo-European deities. For some this may not be an authentically Gaulish approach. That being said, it is the approach I have used, and it has served me quite well.

Learning about Artemis and Diana provided me with a great foundation to understand how I could approach Abnoba. I will discuss them and a few other related goddesses further in a later chapter. For now, I will just say that I looked at their attributes and symbols to see if they could be applied to Abnoba. For many traits this actually served me quite well. Additionally, this work enabled me to discover various aspects of Abnoba that I have since applied different epithets to while honoring Her. This has allowed me to get to know Abnoba in a brand-new light.

Connecting to the Wilds

The world's forests are dwindling away. It is estimated that 10,000 years ago the earth's habitable land was 57% forested (Ritchie and Roser, 2021). We have since lost one-third of our forests. To make matters more dire, half of that loss of land occurred between 8000 BCE and 1900 CE, but the other half has been lost since 1900 (Ritchie and Roser, 2021). That is a dramatic and rapid rate of loss. Knowing this, how is a goddess of the forest relevant in our lives today? I feel that because of this fact Abnoba is more important than ever before. It is imperative that we remember the importance of the forests and strive to protect them at all costs.

The benefits of spending time in the woods are numerous. Some of these benefits include lowering your blood pressure, reducing stress and overall improving your mood (Qing, 2010). Plants give off airborne chemicals called phytoncides. Breathing in this chemical is believed to contribute to these positive reactions. Even just taking a few minutes to sit with a tree can be known to produce some of these effects. This can even include green spaces in our cities.

While some will disagree, I would argue that Abnoba is present to some extent in the city. We just have to look a little harder to find Her. She can be found in the cultivated city parks. She can be found in the random grove of trees on the abandoned city block. Cities are still a part of nature. Sure, they are manmade, but they are still a part of our environment. It just takes more work to find the wilds left in our cities. I find Her presence in every tree I see along the street. Trees are vital to my personal well-being, and a critical element to all of our health.

So, if you can find that one spot, that single tree, where you can sense the divine, you can still connect to Abnoba. However, if you can find a way to explore the mysteries of the forest, I urge you to take the opportunity and go explore.

I do feel that it is important to connect to the wilds of the forest beyond the city limits. I cannot always get away whenever I desire and head out to the woods no matter how much I may want to. In fact, weeks may go by before I can even take a quick walk at a local park. However, I am fortunate in that I own a house and property just outside of the city. I am able to cultivate a bit of wilderness in my backyard, however developed it may truly be. When I do finally get the chance to recharge out in the woods, though, it is as if my entire self is revitalized.

Another method to connect to the forests, and to Abnoba, is by becoming active in the environmental movement, particularly forest conservation. The level of involvement for each of us will vary from person to person as our abilities are unique. The simple act of picking up trash at a local park is one method of involvement. However, some of us are faced with disabilities that make certain options unattainable. Do not let that sway you from honoring Abnoba. If you look hard enough there is bound to be a way that you can contribute. Maybe writing a letter to your congressperson about some upcoming environmental regulations suits you better. Composting and recycling at home are two other simple methods we can take to help. Finding a way to make an impact towards environmental activism really helped me to further connect with Abnoba.

Exploring Other Roles

Abnoba is first and foremost a goddess of the wilds. She is intrinsically connected to the forests, animals, lakes, rivers, mountains and marshes. However, in my own workings I have discovered Her to be a goddess of seemingly opposing roles. She can govern over healing, but also disease. She is a goddess of the hunted and the hunter. She governs the untamed wild, but She is ever present in the tamed countryside. I see Her as a liminal goddess having sway over the boundaries that divide opposing forces.

One of the more interesting roles that She has shown to me is as a goddess of the margins. That is to say She seems to fight for those who are marginalized. People that society has labeled *other*. People who live on what some refer to as the boundaries, or edges, of society. People of a different race than the dominating white culture. People who are not straight or cis gendered. People who are not men. People who are financially disadvantaged. People with mental or physical disabilities. She sees us. She is us.

I must admit that I initially came to understand this role by researching Diana. I learned that Diana was quite fond of slaves and plebeians, as well as women and children. This led to me seeing Diana in a different way besides the common goddess of the hunt motif for which she is known. I started to wonder if Abnoba possessed these traits as well. Then, the more that I began to meditate and pray with Abnoba the more I began to see She did in fact resonate with this role. I cannot be certain if this is how Abnoba was seen in the past, but I know in my experience it is a role that She has decided to take up in our modern world.

I think it is very important to remember that the Gaulish Deuoi possess much more than any single role. Actually, I would say that all deities are more than one defining trait. We tend to limit them to war gods, hunting goddesses, healing gods, etc. They are in fact full of complexities that we seldom get to experience in their full glory. In the same manner that you are more than your job title, the deities are more than their most well-known attributes. Another thing that we need to remember is that, like people, the deities change and evolve. I believe they still hold sway over the aspects that they once did, but the world has changed and so has their purview.

I have personally confirmed these aspects through my own UPG. I feel that too often we read about a deity, and assign their given historical roles to them, to the detriment of our personal experiences. We hesitate to reach out when needing assistance in another area. We tend to look down on the UPG of others. When we do this, we miss the opportunity to discover what else they may be capable of helping out on. So, in essence we severely limit the extent of their influence. When I desired spiritual support during my home remodeling projects, I never would have expected Abnoba to support me from the available information. Upon meditation and prayers, I discovered She was happy to lend me Her spiritual strength with my projects. It was upon further research that I discovered the Roman goddess Diana and her connections to the countryside villa – these were large homesteading estates. Later, I would discover an inscription of Abnoba was actually left at a villa such as this. Taking this into account, and Diana being associated with Abnoba, seemed to shine a light on that comparison.

These roles of Abnoba should not be seen as separate goddesses, but it does help me when reaching out to Abnoba to call upon a certain aspect that would serve to be more beneficial. This helps me focus a bit more on the desired outcome of our interaction. For instance, if I have a friend who is sick, and I wish to reach out for assistance, it would not help much to call on Abnoba as the goddess of the homestead. Instead, I would call on Abnoba as a goddess of healing.

Conclusion

As I have already mentioned, a lot of the conclusions I have reached came about through comparative mythology and personal encounters. When using the comparative method, I applied certain traits in my practice to Abnoba to see what She responded to and what She did not. This allowed me to experience Abnoba as a multifaceted goddess. As this is experimental, and thus controversial, I think it is very important to apply facts to the process as well. For the next chapter I am going to shift the focus to the more concrete evidence that we have in the archeological record. While it is not an abundance of information it certainly did help me on my journey.

Chapter 2

Historical Record

"Maiden Queen of the forests, whose ungentle standards and ruthless warfare I follow, scorning my sex, in no Grecian manner – nor are the barbarous-fashioned Colchians or troops of Amazons more truly thy votaries – if I have never joined revelling bands or the wanton nightly sport, if, although stained by a hated union, I have nevertheless handled not the smooth wands nor the soft skeins, but even after wedlock remained in the rough wilds, a huntress still and in my heart a virgin; if I took no thought to hide my fault in some secret cave, but showed my child and confessed and laid him trembling at thy feet – no puny weakling was he, but straightway crawled to my bow, and as a babe he cried for arrows in his first tearful accents: for him I pray – ah! what mean these nights of terror, these threatening dreams? – for him, who now in confident hope, trusting overmuch, alas, in thee, is gone to battle; grant me to see him victorious in the war, or if I ask too much, grant me but to see him! Here let him labour and bear thy arms. Make the dire signs of ill to cease; what power, O Diana of the woods, have Maenads and Theban deities in our glades? Woe is me! – why in my own heart do I find a dreadful omen in the oak? But if sleep sends true presagings to my unhappy mind, I beseech thee, merciful Dictynna, by thy mother's travail and thy brother's splendour, pierce with all thine arrows this unblest womb! Let him first hear of his wretched mother's death!" Statius Thebaid IX 608-635 (Translation Mozley, J. H)

Abnoba is truly a goddess of the woods and the wilds. She is intrinsically connected to the lands that She roams. Historically, this has been the Black Forest of Germany. I have many ancestors from this region. Unfortunately, I have never had the opportunity to see it for myself. You may be curious how a guy living in the outskirts of a small town in Indiana connected to a goddess that has ties to a land so far away. Personally, I feel that the gods travel with us. They are not stagnant beings. Yes, they may be tied to a specific piece of land, but when those people moved, I feel that the gods also moved with them. After all, the Roman Diana was attached to numerous physical locations, but her worship was spread throughout the Roman Empire. The old gods will find us wherever we may be. Abnoba reached out to me, and I have not looked back.

Origins of Her Name

The first record of Her name actually comes to us from Pliny the Elder in 77 CE in his *'Natural History'*. Here he states,

> *"Passing beyond that spot we come to the mouths of the Ister. This river rises in Germany in the heights of Mount Abnoba, opposite to Rauricum, a town of Gaul, and flow for a course of many miles beyond the Alps and through nations innumerable, under the name of the Danube"* (Translated by Bostock and Riley, 2018, p. 328).

Here, Abnoba is connected right away to a mountain giving it Her name. Next, in 98 CE Tacitus mentions Abnoba in his *'Germania'*. Here he states that,

> *"The Danube, poured from the easy and gently raised ridge of Mount Abnoba, visits several nations in its course, till at length it bursts out by six channels into the Pontic Sea; a seventh is lost in marshes"* (Tacitus).

Again, we have a reference for Her association with the mountains. Further, Ptolemy refers to this same region as the Abnobaei Mountains in his work *'Geography'* written in the second century CE. So, as we can see Abnoba was well established early on as a goddess connected to this region. From this we can ascertain that Abnoba is a goddess of the land and nature. She is especially connected to mountains and the forests.

The meaning of the name Abnoba is actually still up for scholarly debate. The primary school of thought is that the name is related to the Celtic word *abona* meaning 'river' (Delamarre, 2003, p. 1). This would be related to the Old Irish *aba*, Welsh *afon* and Breton *aven* each meaning river. This in turn would stem from the Indo-European root **ab* which signifies 'the waters' (Beck, 2009). So now, in addition to Her connection to mountains and forests She is linked to water features. There is evidence of this root being used on two other occasions. First, in Portugal there is a goddess known from one inscription known as Abna. The other is a goddess from Austria who is known as Abiona. Whether or not these goddesses are related in any significant way we may never know.

Inscriptions

There have been a total of ten inscriptions found thus far bearing the name Abnoba. All of these inscriptions were found in the former Roman Province of Germania Superior, chiefly in and around the region of Germany's Black Forest. Of these inscriptions She is twice referred to as *Diana* Abnoba. I have listed each of the ten inscriptions below, and I have tried to find translations for what I could. I personally do not possess the knowledge to translate the inscriptions. When needed I have cited the translator. Reading these old inscriptions is quite the task in and of itself as they are very old and worn. It may seem confusing to read the text that is in Latin which is why I worked hard to find proper translations. Unfortunately, some are simply too illegible to decipher.

The first inscription that we have is from Stuttgart, Germany. Discovered in 1904 this dedication dates to sometime in between 71 CE and 150 CE. It reads as follows;

'Abnobae / sacrum / M(arcus) Proclinius / Verus stator / v(otum) s(olvit) l(ibens) l(aetus) m(erito)' (CIL XIII, 11746) 'The Abnoba consecrated Marcus Proclinius Verus stator happily and joyfully after his vows fee redeemed' (Horn, 2014).

This next inscription is from Waldmössingen Germany near Schramberg. It is believed to have been found during the construction of a church and was apparently walled back up within the church. It is because of this that only a copy by hand has survived. Due to its condition, I could not locate a proper translation of the text. Additionally, there is no precise record of when it was discovered. It is assumed to date to sometime between 71 CE to 200 CE.

'Abnobae / sacrum / L(ucius) Vennon[i]us / Me[------]' (CIL XIII, 06356)

The following inscription is from Pforzheim in Germany. It seems to be missing some information, and because of this the translation is tentative at best. This one was discovered in 1909 and is believed to date from 171 CE to 230 CE.

'In h(onorem) [d(omus) d(ivinae)---] / Abn[obae---] / quae [stor? ---] / [------]' (CIL XIII, 11721)
'In honor of the divine imperial family, Quae [?-] / ? the Abnoba' (Horn, 2014)

These next three inscriptions I could not find any translations for so I will simply state where they are from and list the text as is. From Pforzheim we have the following found in the villa rustica "Fohlenstallschlößchen." This was found in 1832 and dates between 151 CE and 250 CE. It states;

'[--- Ab] nob (a) e / [- A?] Nulius / [------' (CIL XIII, 06332)

This next one was found in Ubstadt-Weiher, Germany in fragments. This particular find has since been lost. It is reported to have read as follows;

'[I(n) h(onorem)] d(omus) d(ivinae) / [D]ean (a)e A[bnob(a)e] / [---] viu [s? ---] / [------?]' (CIL XIII, 06342)

The following inscription is another one from Stuttgart that states;

'[A]bn[oba e] / [s]a[crum?] / [------]' (CIL XIII, 11747)

This next dedication is from Mühlburg and it is special because it is engraved on the base of a statue of Abnoba. Unfortunately, the statue is missing its head, but we can see that she is dressed in a short tunic similar to ones depicting Diana. However, she is a bit stockier than most images of Diana, perhaps reflecting a stockier build of the Gauls themselves. She is also wearing boots in this statue as Her right hand reaches for Her quiver tied up on Her back. By Her feet is a dog holding a hare in its paws.

'Deae Abnoba(e) / Lucius Moderatus v(otum) s (olvit) (l.) m(erito)' (CIL XIII, 06326)
'To the Goddess Abnoba Lucius Moderatus paid his vow willingly and deservedly' (Beck, 2009).

We have a rather lengthy dedication in this next inscription. This one was found in 1825 and dates to around 90 CE to 96 CE. It states;

'Abnoba e / Q(uintus) Antonius / Silo | (centurio) leg(ionis) I a / diutricis et / leg(ionis) II adiutri / cis et leg(ionis) III

Aug(ustae) / et leg(ionis) IIII F (laviae) f(elicis) / et leg(ionis) XI C (laudiae) p (iae) f(idelis) / et leg(ionis) XXII p(iae) f(idelis) D(omitianae) / v(otum) s(olvit) l(ibens) l(aetus) m(erito)' (CIL XIII, 06357)
'The Abnoba Quintus Antonius Silo, captain of the Legio I adiutrix, Legio III Augusta, Legio IIII Flavia felix, Legio XI Claudia pia fidelis and the Legio XXII pia fidelis Domitiana made his vows happy and having redeemed for a fee' (Horn, 2014).

In these last two inscriptions Abnoba is directly referred to with the name Diana. This speaks to the similarities that these two probably possess. The first one comes from Badenweiler, Germany at the thermal springs there. Noemie Beck mentions that while his first name, Marcus, is of Latin origin his nomen is of Celtic origin. This signifies that the dedicator was connected to his Gaulish roots (Beck, 2009). The dating of this dedication ranges from 71 CE to 250 CE and was discovered in 1784. The finding of this inscription at a thermal spring has led many to assert Abnoba has connections to a healing cult, at least at this particular site.

'Dianae Abnob[ae] M(arcus) Senn[i]us [F]ronto s(olvit?) L(ibens?) ex voto' (CIL XIII, 05334)
'To Diana Abnoba, Marcus Sennius Fronto offered (this altar)' (Beck, 2009).

This final dedication from Mühlenbach, Germany dates to 193 CE and was discovered in 1778. Here it states;

'In h(onorem) d(omus) d(ivinae) / Deanae Abn/obae Cassia/ nus Casati / v. (otum) s. (olvit) l. (ibens) l. (aetus) m. (erito) / et Attianus / frater Fal / con (e) et Claro / co(n)s(ulibus)' (CIL XIII, 06283)

'To honor of divine Imperial house to have the Diana Abnoba Cassiannus, of Cassatus Son, and Attianus, the brothers, glad and joyful, how our self befits you vow fulfills, under the consuls Falco and Clarus' (Horn, 2014).

All of these dedications go to show what an important goddess Abnoba was during this time, particularly in the region of the Black Forest. We also learned from the statue that She has some role related to hunting, wild animals and dogs. Finally, we know that She was at least tangentially connected to Diana. Unfortunately, we do not have any more information to inform us on an archeological level.

Investigation

Now we must investigate this evidence to help inform us of what we can to learn about Abnoba. The first piece of information we have is Her name. If Her name does indeed reflect a connection to rivers, we can safely assume She is a river goddess. I have come to associate Her with all fresh water systems such as lakes, marshes and of course rivers. We also know that Her name was attached to the entire region of the Black Forest. This includes the rivers, mountains, forests and I think we could safely assume the animals that reside there.

Additionally, we learned that at least in one location she is tied to a healing thermal spring. This makes sense as the water and healing are very integrated in the Gaulish worldview. There are several healing goddesses in Gaul connected to springs, such as Damona and Sirona. It is interesting to note that the former two goddesses are also connected to the Gaulish gods Borvo and Grannos who are themselves associated with Apollo. Whether or not Abnoba was connected to a Gaulish 'Apollo' we do not know, but the possibility is intriguing. It is also possible that at other locations Abnoba had connections to healing as well, but for now the most we can do is guess.

Perhaps the biggest piece of the puzzle to understanding Abnoba is Her connection to the Roman goddess Diana. We are able to see that in two locations this title is given to Abnoba. As a goddess tied to the wild landscape this makes perfect sense. Looking at the statue we see many similarities to Diana. Her quiver and the dog with the hare in its paw would definitely indicate a goddess connected to the hunt.

Likewise, this connection to Diana could also reflect a connection to Artemis. Both Diana and Artemis were also linked to healing like their brother Apollo. This is further proof of a connection to healing for Abnoba. The sphere of influence of Diana and Artemis is far greater than mere goddesses of the hunt. To understand Abnoba it is vital that we compare and contrast Her with other goddesses that we know to be similar. This is not to say that they are the same. I am a polytheist and I thoroughly believe each god and goddess is a unique being with their own agency. That being said, the comparative method can be very useful. As we can see the Romans felt that Abnoba carried similar enough traits with Diana for them to refer to Her with that moniker. So, if we examine traits of these other goddesses, it helps paint a more vivid picture of Abnoba.

Conclusion

While we are not flooded with information on the historical record, we do now have a decent picture of Abnoba. As far as the number of inscriptions go, we are actually quite fortunate. Some gods and goddesses we only have a name left for us to decipher their roles in our world. To have ten dedications along with a statue really helps our understanding of Her. In the next chapter we will dive a little deeper by looking into other goddesses that have a similar scope of influence as Abnoba. We will use this information to build on what we learned in this chapter. Hopefully, this will provide a better understanding of Abnoba.

Chapter 3

Related Goddesses

"I sing of Artemis, whose shafts are of gold, who cheers on the hounds, the pure maiden, shooter of stags, who delights in archery, own sister to Apollo with the golden sword. Over the shadowy hills and windy peaks she draws her golden bow, rejoicing in the chase, and sends out grievous shafts. The tops of the high mountains tremble and the tangled wood echoes awesomely with the outcry of beasts: earth quakes and the sea also where fishes shoal. But the goddess with a bold heart turns every way destroying the race of wild beasts: and when she is satisfied and has cheered her heart, this huntress who delights in arrows slackens her supple bow and goes to the great house of her dear brother Phoebus Apollo, to the rich land of Delphi, there to order the lovely dance of the Muses and Graces. There she hangs up her curved bow and her arrows, and heads and leads the dances, gracefully arrayed, while all they utter their heavenly voice, singing how neat-ankled Leto bare children supreme among the immortals both in thought and in deed. Hail to you, children of Zeus and rich-haired Leto! And now I will remember you and another song also." Homeric Hymn 27 to Artemis (Translation: Evelyn-White, H. G. p. 453)

In the last chapter we discussed the archaeological information available about Abnoba. In this chapter we are going to shift our focus a bit to the Classical World of Greece and Rome and investigate Diana and Artemis. I am sure it may seem counterproductive to change the focus of the book to these two goddesses so early in the book. However, I feel it is critical to understand these two goddesses to truly begin to know Abnoba. I will also briefly discuss a few other goddesses who may share some similarities with Abnoba.

Diana

The name Diana is related to the Latin word dīus meaning 'godly'. This can only go to show what a lofty position she held in the Roman pantheon. While she was an indigenous goddess among the Romans Her identity was soon connected with the Greek Artemis. Her iconic connection to the Moon probably did not come about until this correlation began.

Roles

The most well-known domain of Diana is that of the goddess of the hunt. Most everyone is aware of Diana in this role. As a goddess of the hunt, she is tied to all things wild including the animals such as deer. However, she also has connections to domesticated animals, especially the dog as a constant companion to the hunter. In art Diana is frequently depicted with deer and hounds.

Over time Diana became increasingly bound to the countryside as well. This is a much tamer role than that of the wild huntress, but Diana is a complex and multifaceted goddess. She was especially given reverence at the *villa rustica*. A villa rustica was the name used to represent a villa that was in the countryside. This villa was often at the center of a large farm. This is another interesting link to Abnoba who had a dedication given to Her at least once at a villa rustica.

Another popular association of Diana is that of fertility and childbirth. She is known to protect mothers during childbirth and to protect the children thereafter. It is in this role that she would occasionally be called Diana Lucina. This is a title also frequently given to Juno. It was common practice to leave offerings of terracotta shaped babies at her shrines. While there have not been any finds of terracotta babies at dedication sites of Abnoba, you could infer that she may indeed share in this guise.

A little-known role of Diana was that of a household goddess. While it is not her most common aspect it is present. Each house of ancient Rome was protected by a *lar*. Individual people and places were watched over by the *genius*. The *penates* would typically concern themselves with the pantry or storeroom of the home. Statuettes representing these figures would be placed in the *lararium*, most commonly a niche in the wall. Frequently, the household would also have a patron deity that was honored in the lararium as well. There has been evidence that in Pompeian homes some of this worship was indeed given to Diana (Descoeudres, 1994).

As a goddess of woman and children we begin to see a pattern in those that she holds dear. She was also connected to the lower classes like the plebeians, but especially slaves. Her biggest festival in the Roman calendar was the Ides of August on the 13th and it was called the Nemoralia. This was especially regarded as a holiday for the slaves. It is said that slaves could even receive asylum at her temples. It is in this regard that we can look to Diana as a goddess of the margins looking after those that society treats less than fair.

Associated Deities

The first deity that is connected to Diana would have to be her twin brother Apollo. They are both the children of Jupiter and Latona. The introduction of Apollo to Rome may have spurred the initial connection between Diana and Artemis. Apollo was the bright god of the sun and so Diana, his twin, became the goddess of the moon. They both also shared in having healing attributes.

As a triple goddess, Diana was related to both Luna and Hecate. This trinity was usually considered to be Diana as the huntress, Diana as the moon, and Diana of the underworld. The name of her in this guise was Diana Triformis. Because of Her link to Hecate in this role she was also referred to as Trivia. This title refers specifically to Diana's role as a guardian of roadways. More specifically three-way crossroads as this often signified a connection to the underworld.

Sacred Sites

One of Diana's early connections was with Egeria and Virbius. Egeria was a water nymph who, like Diana, was a guardian of childbirth. Virbius was connected to the woodlands, a role which he shared with Diana. Virbius is the equivalent of the Greek Hippolytus. The chief center of this cult was at Aricia, which was located on the shores of a volcanic lake that was known as the *Mirror of Diana* (Price & Kearns, 2003. p. 163). This temple was located in a sacred grove, or *nemus* which is a cognate of the Gaulish word with a similar meaning *nemeton* (Delamarre, 2003, p. 17). Here she was called Diana *Nemorensis* meaning 'Diana of the Wood'. The site was dedicated to Her by Egerius Baebius of Tusculum who was a leader of the Latins. The priest at this site was known as *rex nemorensis* meaning 'king of the grove'. This priest was unique among other officials of Rome in that he was an escaped slave who had killed his predecessor (Price & Kearns, 2003. p. 468).

Another shrine was located in southern Italy on Mt. Tifata. This name means 'holm-oak grove' (Price & Kearns, 2003. p. 163). Here she was called Diana Tifantina. As a goddess of the wood and wilderness this is an appropriate name. The area also included estates, probably worked by slaves. This harkens back to what I previously discussed regarding Diana and her strong connection to slaves. Additionally, this brings to mind the locations of the dedications to Abnoba which were mostly isolated to the wilderness of the Black Forest region of Germania Superior.

In Rome, Diana had an important temple on the Aventine hill. This temple was probably preceded by an altar. The site has connections with the Latin League. The Latin League was an alliance of Latin groups that joined together to oppose Etruscan Rome near the end of the 6th century BCE.

From the above information we can gather several possibilities of the aspects Abnoba may possess. I think we can officially confirm from the evidence that Abnoba is a goddess of the hunt, the wilderness, and animals. Additionally, if She is truly connected to Diana, She was probably linked to the countryside, women, children, slaves or those who held a lower status in society in general. Now we will turn to Artemis and see if we can learn even more.

Artemis

So much of what we know about Roman Diana comes from her being conflated with the Greek Artemis. In understanding Artemis, we can further learn about the complexities of these two great goddesses. Her name is of uncertain origins and may in fact be a pre-Greek name. Like Diana, Artemis was a goddess of the moon, the hunt, and childbirth. As we will learn she held numerous roles among the Greeks.

Roles

The many roles of Artemis are probably best expressed by exploring her epithets. One such epithet that was occasionally applied to her is Potnia Theron meaning 'Mistress of the Animals' (Price & Kearns, 2003. p. 59). While she was known as the goddess of the hunt Artemis was also known to protect animals, in particular the young. Along this same path Artemis was a goddess greatly aligned with nature. She was a goddess of trees, lakes, marshes, and just about any other wild place.

Artemis was a goddess of women, especially during transformative times in their life. She aided women from parthenos (virgin) to adulthood, especially during childbirth. She would be called Artemis Brauron or Munichia when guiding women through these transitions. When protecting women during childbirth specifically she was known as Artemis Eileithyia. In addition, she was concerned with men going through rites of passage like the transition to adulthood. Not to mention her overseeing their actions during the hunt and occasionally even wartime.

She is also known to bring about sudden death particularly to women just as her brother, Apollo, did for men. One of the myths of Artemis is that involving Callisto. She punished Callisto for sleeping with Zeus by transforming her into a bear and then shooting Callisto with an arrow instantly killing her. Another popular myth concerned the great hunter, Actaeon. He had accidentally come upon Artemis bathing and she subsequently transformed him into a stag. After taking this form he was torn apart by his own hounds.

Associated Deities

Artemis was very close with her twin brother Apollo. In some tales Artemis was the first born. While her birth went accordingly her mother, Leto, was in labor with Apollo for nine nights and nine days. It was said that Artemis served as her mother's midwife during this process. As Apollo took on the byname of Phoebus, Artemis had the moniker of Phoebe bestowed upon her.

Like Diana, Artemis was connected to the Greek Moon goddess Selene. Her identification with Selene is believed to be a late occurrence. It may have coincided with the Thracian goddess, Bendis, being brought into Greece. We will discuss Bendis a little bit later. This role as a Moon goddess was also probably influenced by her brother Apollo being associated with the Sun. Another goddess who Artemis was closely linked to was Hekate. In particular, her connection with Hekate occurred with the addition of Selene where the three formed a triad just like the one of the Roman Diana, Hecate and Luna.

Other Associations

Among sacred objects of Artemis, the bow and arrow take center stage. She was seldom seen without this weapon. She was first given her bow and arrow by the Kyklopes (Cyclopes). Artemis was also known for her golden chariot that was drawn by deer whose antlers shined of gold. They were larger than bulls and she had found them herding along the river Anauros.

Several plants were also sacred to Artemis. Both the palm tree and the cypress tree were held with great reverence by Artemis. The palm and cypress were connected to Artemis and Apollo as it was linked to their births. Amaranth was also highly regarded particularly through her cult at Amaranthos.

Animals are very important in the lore of Artemis. The deer have already been mentioned, but it is worth bringing them up again due to their high status held by Artemis. As a huntress, hounds were also given reverence. She received her hunting dogs from Pan. Finally, the bear was tied to Artemis particularly at Brauron where a festival took place honoring Artemis along with the bear. There young girls aged around five to ten would play the part of arktoi (bears). This served to turn them from children to marriageable maidens (Price & Kearns, 2003. p. 60).

As you can see, many of the aspects of Artemis are the same as those of Diana. When researching the two it was often hard to keep track of which goddess was being referred to. Especially in sources where their names are used interchangeably.

Next, we will venture far north of Greece to the Baltic lands. We do not possess a lot of information on the Balts like we do for the Greeks and Romans so I am afraid the information will be brief. Still, I thought it was important to look at this source as it provides more information about another woodland goddess.

Medeina

Medeina is a Baltic goddess of the hunt. Her name comes from the words *medis* meaning 'tree,' and *mede* meaning 'forest' (Gimbutas, 1999. p. 210). Early on she was equated with Diana so much so that she is even called Diana in some early accounts. She was intimately connected to the forest and the wilds. Her special animal was the hare. She was considered a single goddess who refused to marry. One significant difference from Diana was that

Medeina did not help the hunters, but instead she would protect the animals from being hunted. It has been said that her precious hare would help to lead the hunters astray. In fact, there is even a tale that the Lithuanian king, Mindaugas, would even avoid hunting in a forest should he come across the hare of Medeina (Gimbutas, 1999. p. 210).

The commonalities of Medeina with both Artemis and Diana are quite apparent. I was most interested though in the major difference of Medeina between those two. That is to say her role as a protector *from* the hunters. As a non-hunter I prefer to see Abnoba in this light. This is not to say that if you are a hunter that Abnoba disapproves. I want to make it clear that I do not believe that. In fact, I would go so far as to say that hunting is a sacred act to Abnoba, but it goes beyond just the sport of slaughtering animals. I think she still demands respect for the animal whose life is taken. For myself, Abnoba acts as a goddess who protects wildlife and she holds their lives in high regard. That is just how she presents Herself to me. Again, this is my UPG. You may be a hunter that feels Abnoba is your guide, and I think that is a perfectly valid experience.

Now we will turn back to Southern Europe once again. This time just north of Greece to Ancient Thrace. Not much is known about the Thracians, but we do have fragments of their religious beliefs. They are also descendants of the Indo-European peoples so I felt that it was important to briefly mention their hunting goddess here as well.

Bendis

Bendis was a Thracian goddess whose cult spread into Greece between 430 and 412 BCE (Price & Kearns, 2003. p. 84). She was linked to the goddess Artemis and was frequently depicted in Greek art wearing boots just as Artemis wore. She had a festival called the Bendideia. There, Thracians and Athenians would engage in torch-races on horseback. The festivities would last all through the night. The event would take place at her sanctuary located at Piraeus in Attica. The festivals of Bendis were quite wild and Strabo refers to them as orgiastic (Price & Kearns, 2003. p. 84). Her cult was frequently blended with another Thracian goddess, Cotys, who also had wild events dedicated to her.

While we do not gather a lot of information relevant to Abnoba, we do learn that a wild festival was held. This, in combination with what we will learn about the festivals to Artemis, show how important celebration was to honoring these woodland goddesses. We do have one interesting link and that is torches. Torches are important to Bendis, Artemis and Diana. Based on this, and a personal connection to be referenced later, I feel it is safe to assume that they may have some significance to Abnoba as well. We now shift our focus out of Europe and into Asia. Here we come across another culture with some Indo-Europeans roots. They have their own goddess of the wilds that we will discuss below.

Aranyani

Aranyani is from the Indian subcontinent. While the other goddesses thus far are from Europe, Aranyani does have connections to the other goddesses through her Indo-European origins. She may in fact be one of the oldest recorded forest goddesses having been found in the Rig Veda, the oldest known Sanskrit text. It was most likely compiled between 1500 and 1000 BCE. The hymn that is dedicated to her will be included at the beginning of the following chapter. Aranyani is thought to be very brave as she endures life alone in the forest which can be seen as a very treacherous place. She is particularly known for the ability to feed man and beast without tilling the land, meaning she supplies food from the forest.

Due to the age of the origins of Aranyani we can see the importance of woodland goddesses to the Indo-European peoples. Comparing Aranyani to Abnoba we can possibly see

Abnoba as a provider of food once again. This time it is not just animals, but She provides the fruits and nuts of the forest. Although Aranyani is praised for the ability to provide food without the tilling of land, I feel that tilling the land to provide food is still under the care of Abnoba. As a goddess of the countryside, where people commonly did grow their own food, this makes a lot of sense. Not to mention the foods we grow today were once found in the forest and field. Maybe learning how to cultivate this food was a gift from Abnoba so that we may learn to provide for ourselves.

Conclusion

I hope you have learned a bit about these 'sister' goddesses (as I like to call them) of Abnoba. I will be using a significant amount of the information from these goddesses to create a fuller picture of Abnoba. From their attributes, symbols, festivals and sharing Indo-European roots it could be safe to assume that they share some traits. In my personal work with Abnoba this has been most useful in really getting to know Her. I hope it is just as useful to you as it has been for me.

Chapter 4

Epithets and Symbols

"Goddess of wild and forest who seemest to vanish from the sight.
How is it that thou seekest not the village? Art thou not afraid?
What time the grasshopper replies and swells the shrill cicala's voice,
Seeming to sound with tinkling bells, the Lady of the Wood exults.
And, yonder, cattle seem to graze, what seems a dwelling-place
appears:
Or else at eve the Lady of the Forest seems to free the wains.
Here one is calling to his cow, another there hath felled a tree:
At eve the dweller in the wood fancies that somebody hath screamed.
The Goddess never slays, unless some murderous enemy approach.
Man eats of savoury fruit and then takes, even as he wills, his rest.
Now have I praised the Forest Queen, sweet-scented, redolent of
balm,
The Mother of all sylvan things, who tills not but hath stores of
food."
Hymn CXLVI to Aranyani

The last chapter served many purposes, but it specifically
worked to inform our practice concerning the next two chapters.
Many of the epithets and symbols that will be discussed here
are greatly influenced by Greco-Roman sources. I want to stress
that I am not simply turning Abnoba into the Gaulish Artemis
or Diana. I am drawing conclusions from the available evidence
to understand a goddess for whom we unfortunately lack a lot
of information. I experimented with these various epithets and
found that they worked for me.

Epithets
The following epithets will be in Gaulish followed by an English

translation. I must admit here that I am in no way a linguist. I am very fortunate in the fact that I had help from a friend with these translations. These are the terms that I use in my personal work and they have served me quite well. I hope that they can be of help to you as well.

Dêuâ Allatês 'Goddess of the Wilds'

The title Dêuâ Allatês means 'Goddess of the Wilds'. This comes from the Gaulish word *dêuâ* meaning 'goddess' and *alattus* meaning 'wild'. This could perhaps be the most established of the epithets. Abnoba and Her connection to Diana, the locations of Her cult sites, and the hare, dog and quiver that She is shown with all point to a goddess who could be associated with this title. This is the chief role of the goddesses referenced in the last chapter and I find no reason that it should be disputed. This is the role I am most familiar with Abnoba. Every time I venture off into the woods it is this aspect that I call to. There are several other natural environments that I feel called to Abnoba in this aspect.

One place that I particularly connect to Abnoba in this role is in wetlands. Similar in character to Diana Heleia, or 'Diana of the Marshes' I feel that Abnoba is very present in this biome. It is safe to assume that Abnoba is connected to water as She appears to be attached to both rivers and springs. I do not feel like it is a leap to associate Her with marshes, wetlands and lakes. In fact, in my dealings with Abnoba I sense that She has passion for all freshwater ecosystems. This is also heavily based on my own UPG as I live near a few wetlands that I associate specifically with Abnoba. I feel Her presence almost immediately at these locations when I arrive there. The first time that I experienced Abnoba here was one of the earlier instances that I recognized that it was indeed Her. Any time that I feel particularly disconnected I can go to these locations and feel instantly rejuvenated.

Riganâ Milon 'Queen of the Animals'

This term is composed of two elements; *rigana* meaning 'queen' and *milo* meaning 'animal' (Delamarre, 2003. pp. 17 & 20). This gives us something akin to 'Queen of the Animals', and is partially influenced from the epithet of Artemis *Potnia Theron*, or 'Lady/Queen of the Beasts'. We can make the safe assumption that Abnoba is a goddess of the hunt. We understand this because of the locations of Her worship, Her attire, the hound that accompanies Her, and Her identification with Diana. One can imagine Her ruling over dogs, deer, rabbits, boars, bears, etc. If, like Diana and Artemis, She is also a goddess of the countryside and rural life then she is probably associated with domesticated farm animals as well. The cow, sheep, and goats may all fall under Her domain, as well as their wild counterparts the extinct Auroch (cow), Mouflon (sheep), and the various wild Capra (goats) species.

If you desire you could also honor Abnoba as the huntress in this role. As previously stated, I am personally not a hunter so this is not a role with which I work. I am sure you are wondering why someone who does not hunt honors a goddess of the hunt. In my personal experience I see Abnoba similar to Medeina in that She leads hunters astray to protect wild animals. However, that should not stop you from honoring Her as a goddess of the hunt if you so desire. I would venture to say that Abnoba was indeed honored as a huntress in the past, that aspect just does not serve a purpose in my workings. Additionally, as an animist, I see the pivotal role that Abnoba plays in this particular area. She is the protector of the hunter and the hunted. She sees the inherent spirit that exists in both people and non-human animals. She is the boundary between the wild animal and the 'tamed' person.

Caruogenetâ 'Deer Maiden'

The epithet comes from *caruos* meaning 'deer' and *geneta* meaning 'young girl' as in maiden (Delamarre, 2003. pp. 7 & 13).

This gives us 'Deer Maiden'. In truth, this aspect is very closely associated with the previous one. I feel that the connection of Abnoba to the Deer is significant enough to warrant its own title. On several occasions throughout the year, I specifically honor Abnoba as the Deer Maiden. Where I am from the White-tailed Deer is the largest animal around. It is a regal animal and as such I feel it deserves respect. I feel that they are under the strict protection of Abnoba.

Dêuâ Antî **'Goddess of Boundaries'**

Here we once again have dêuâ meaning 'goddess' along with *anto* meaning 'boundary' giving us 'Goddess of Boundaries' (Delamarre, 2003. p. 2). The intersection of the wilds and the civilized is a place where you can find Abnoba. The countryside is one such location. The darkest depths of the forest are what She is well known for, but she is ever-present on the edge of the forest too. As previously stated, She is the boundary between person and animal during the hunt. She protects the animals from undue harm while simultaneously protecting the hunter from the forest predators. Abnoba is a surviving link from our hunter-gatherer past and our current urbanized existence.

She is also a goddess of the cross-roads in this role. This links Her to not only Artemis/Diana, but to Hekate as well. The cross-roads are a liminal association linked with death, as at a three-way cross-road one road can often lead, at least symbolically, to the underworld. Additionally, this further links Her to the role as a goddess of death. She is at the border of the living and the dead. This is a role of which I am very familiar. She has warned me of the impending deaths of several close relatives. In addition, She has guided me through the deaths of these very important people in my life.

Finally, I see this aspect as representative of those of us who may be seen as being on the boundaries of society. The people that live on the periphery of the dominant white cisgender culture that pervades our communities. There are a number of groups that this could include. For instance, women would fit under this umbrella. While I am not a woman, I still call to Abnoba in this role. It is most beneficial when saying prayers of good health or well wishes to the women that are in my life. I see Abnoba concerned with everyone, but I do imagine She plays a special part in a woman's life. People of color and the LGBTQ+ community would also be under the guidance of Abnoba as Dêuâ Antî. Finally, children would be under Her protection as well. As the most innocent persons of our society, I feel that Abnoba takes a special interest in protecting children.

Dêuâ Iaccî 'Goddess of Health'

This title comes from *iaccos* meaning 'healthy' (Delamarre, 2003, p. 13). Her name would thus be 'Goddess of Health'. This is a role that I was not aware of until doing further research on Abnoba. When I discovered her inscription found at a healing spring, I must say I was initially a bit surprised. However, this aspect does make sense as Diana was also associated with healing. As a goddess of plants, I needed to remind myself that this includes healing plants and herbs as well. Many modern medicines came about by learning the abilities of plants from the field and forest after all. I personally suffer from several health issues and I have come to pray to Abnoba about them on a number of occasions. While I cannot say I have been instantaneously healed, I do feel that she has a vested interest in my overall well-being. I make a lot of healing herbal balms and it is Her that I keep in mind when making them, and when applying them.

Argantoleucâ 'Silver Light'

This name essentially means the 'silver light' and is a reference to the Moon. This is not to say She is *the* Moon, but she is a goddess associated with the Moon. I was hesitant to make the leap of associating Abnoba with the Moon. This role was a later development of both Artemis and Diana so there is little evidence to confirm that Abnoba was linked to the Moon as well. However, I began to make offerings to Abnoba on full moon's and it has been well received. I personally associate the Moon with healing and as we have seen, this is a role I consider closely related to Abnoba too. Besides, Diana was linked to the Moon long before the Romans associated Abnoba with Diana. This means it is possible that Abnoba had this aspect too which helped lead to their conflation among the Romans.

Dêuâ Sterî 'Goddess of the Homestead'

The last epithet that I work with comes from the Gaulish word *stero* meaning 'homestead' giving us 'Goddess of the Homestead' (Delamarre, 2003, 22). While I do not consider Abnoba a hearth and home goddess so to speak, I do encounter Her as being concerned with the homestead as a whole. This initially came from my understanding of Diana and her association with the villas in the countryside. These villas are intermediates between the wild and the urban. While I definitely see Abnoba being associated primarily with the wild I also experience Her as a goddess of the liminal, the in between, and the margins. I feel that homesteading has a place in Her heart. The various activities that are involved in homesteading seem to be under Her watch. I am a homesteader in the most limited definition, but I work to be one more fully someday. I garden, make soap, weave and do various oddities such as this. Unfortunately, some minor physical and mental health impairments limit what I can and cannot take on. However, I still feel guided in my pursuits by Abnoba.

Symbols

As with the aforementioned epithets the following symbols are taken mostly from our knowledge of Diana and Artemis. I will also examine the one statue that we have as that supplies us with a little bit of information as well. Additionally, some of this is informed from my personal practice. These are conclusions I have come to in my dealings with Abnoba.

Bow and Arrow

I feel that we can safely assume the importance of the bow and arrow to Abnoba. Not only is this a common weapon of hunters, but in the one statue we have of Her the quiver is in Her possession. We know that the bow and arrow is the most important weapon to both Diana and Artemis as well. It is possible that like Artemis, Abnoba is able to kill instantly with one shot from Her arrow.

Quiver

The quiver is a critical piece of information that we can use for confirmation of other traits that Abnoba may possess. This allows us to assume She is a goddess of the hunt. This really helps us to draw numerous conclusions as to Her other attributes. We would not be able to assume She uses a bow and arrow at all if it was not for Her quiver. It is an immediate identifier that links Her to Diana and Artemis as well.

Hunting Spear

We do not have any conclusive evidence that Abnoba carries a spear. We do know that Diana and Artemis used one however. Again, as a huntress this is another conclusion that we can possibly draw.

Torch

Once again, we defer to Diana/Artemis and even Bendis. In Rome the sacred festival of Diana was the Nemoralia, or the Festival of Torches. Carrying a torch is one of the traits that links Diana/ Artemis with Hecate/Hekate. Artemis is depicted several times with a torch in hand. I see this as important to Artemis as a light-bringer and her connection to cross-roads and the underworld. In this role she was also referred to as Trivia. Bendis, the Thracian goddess of the hunt, was also celebrated by torch processions. This may be a big leap as we lack concrete evidence that Abnoba has these same roles, but it is one I feel comfortable making. In my personal experience this is indeed an object of importance that She utilizes. I feel that the torch is relevant to Her role as a goddess of the crossroads and underworld. It was a highly personal experience that led me to this assumption, but a very strong one that confirmed this aspect for myself.

Chariot

Numerous gods and goddesses are known for their chariots. Norse Freyja has her cat-drawn chariot. Thor had his goat-drawn chariot. Artemis had one drawn by deer. Again, this is conjecture. I have yet to personally see Her in such a chariot, but I believe that if myths were allowed to develop among the Gauls then we just may have had stories of Her glorious chariot drawn by does, or perhaps stags.

Crown/Head-band/Bonnet

Several depictions of Gaulish goddesses are shown with differing items on their heads. The Matres and Matronae are depicted with head-bands, bonnets, or some other forms of headdresses. Both Rosmerta and Nantosuelta are seen wearing a diadem. In Greek myth, Artemis is shown variously as wearing a crown, head-band, bonnet and even an animal-pelt cap. While we do have one statue of Abnoba it is unfortunately headless. Still, I feel it is a safe assumption to make that She too wore something upon Her head.

Dog

It has been seen, in the one remaining image we have of Her, that the dog is a companion to Abnoba. As a goddess of animals, having a dog is not a far stretch. Likewise, as a huntress this can also be assumed. This is a bond I share with Abnoba. I do not feel like I would be myself without a dog by my side. They are indeed the best friends of *human*kind. We can also determine other interesting links with the dog. In the ancient world dogs were frequently connected to both healing and the underworld. I feel that this only goes to reinforce Abnoba and these two roles.

Deer

Abnoba is not depicted with a deer in the one statue that we have of Her. Nor is there any mention of deer in the inscriptions. That being said, deer are perhaps the most prominent association I have of Abnoba, along with the dog and the rabbit. As deer are most active at dawn and dusk, we see another connection to Abnoba. These are liminal times, neither night nor day, as such they are linked to Abnoba as a goddess of the boundaries. Every time that I spot a deer I feel as though I am catching a slight glimpse of the divine. We know that deer are very important to both Artemis and Diana so this seems like a fair assumption. They are such magnificent animals. Where I am from the White-tailed Deer is the common deer found. They are quite abundant in my region, but it is still awe-inspiring when I manage to catch a glimpse of one.

Wolf

The wolf is one of the icons of the wilderness. Unfortunately, we have eliminated them from much of their natural range. They still remain emblematic representations of the forest though. As Diana was linked with wolves as a forest goddess, I feel it is safe to assume that for Abnoba as well. We know that the dog was a companion of Abnoba and the wolf is the dog's wild ancestor.

Rabbit/Hare

Besides the dog we also have proof of the hare having at least loose associations with Abnoba. Greek historian Arrian makes reference to the Gauls using hounds to flush out hares and into traps (Green, 1992. Pg. 50). The hare in this case may have been Her victim of the hunt. However, like the complex figures of Artemis, Diana and Medeina, She could just as easily be its protector. Perhaps the rabbit is even like the companion of Medeina that leads hunters astray.

Bear

The connection of the bear with Abnoba comes from comparative myth as well as UPG. The bear is the largest carnivore of Europe. The history of people honoring the bear reaches back far into the past. The goddess Artio, whose name derives from the word bear, is obviously associated with the bear as well. The bear is so iconic of the forest that it would be hard to imagine a goddess of the woodlands not being linked to the bear.

Heron

The heron is associated with Artemis in art. There seemed to be a natural link between Abnoba and the heron for me as well. The heron is often seen as the king, or queen, of the marshland. Due to this it is a natural assumption for me to associate Abnoba, who I connect with marshes, to herons as well. They are very regal birds that really do feel like the aristocracy among the wetlands; especially the Great Blue Herons of my bioregion. In addition to herons, I also associate Abnoba with the Sandhill Crane and Whooping Crane.

Turkey Vulture

The link between Abnoba and the turkey vulture is one I have made on my own. The turkey vulture does not hunt. However, they are nature's clean-up crew, especially around where I am from. They form a vital part of the circle of life out in the wild. It is because of this that I hold them as sacred to Abnoba. They are also tied to death as they are scavengers. I feel this is an additional connection to Abnoba in Her guise as Dêuâ Antî, or 'Goddess of Boundaries'.

Coyote

The coyote is another animal that I associate with Abnoba purely through UPG. There are no coyotes in Europe so She was certainly not historically connected to them. However, where I am from, coyotes are apex predators. They are a common feature of both the countryside and the forests. Interestingly these icons of the American wild are becoming more and more common in the cities as well. I look to them to see how nature is interwoven into our towns. They are living proof that 'nature' does not stop at the city limits.

Squirrel

Perhaps the animal that most represents the city and its wild sectors is the squirrel. If there is a tree the chances are good that a squirrel is nearby. Squirrels are nature's forest regenerators. While they may do so unintentionally, the seeds and nuts they bury often grow into trees. These small members of the rodent family are quite happy in towns, villages, cities and the deep forests. They have learned to coexist with us while keeping their wild behavior. I feel that they make excellent ambassadors of the forests, and thus Abnoba.

Animals of the Homestead

The cow, sheep, goat, pig and chicken are very common animals on the farm and homestead. As a goddess of animals, and a goddess of the homestead, these animals have a connection to Abnoba twice over.

Oak & Maple

This is a purely local and personal association. The forests around my parts would not be what they are without the majestic oak and the hearty maple trees. As they make up much of the forests around me, they seem like natural trees to associate with Abnoba. This should go without saying that I truly see all trees as an expression of Abnoba.

Conclusion

As you can see, while we may not have many associations officially attested, we can still make many assumptions. All we can do after that is work these things into our practice and see how Abnoba responds to them. Through your own work you may find many other associations for Abnoba. You will only find out through your own experimentation.

Chapter 5

Sacred Festivals

"Hear me, O queen, Zeus' daughter of many names, Titanic and Bacchic, revered, renowned archer, Torch-bearing goddess bringing light to all, Diktynna, helper at childbirth, you help women in labor, though you know not what labor is. O Frenzy-loving huntress, you loosen girdles and drive distress away; swift arrow-pouring goddess of the outdoors, you roam in the night. Fame-bringing and affable, redeeming and masculine in appearance, Orthia, goddess of swift birth, you are a nurturer of mortal youths, immortal and yet of this earth, you slay wild beasts, O blessed one, your realm is in the mountain forest, you hunt deer. O revered and mighty queen of all, fair blossomed, eternal, sylvan, dog-loving, many-shaped lady of Kydonia, come, dear goddess, as savior to all the initiates, accessible to all, bringing forth the beautiful fruit of the earth, lovely peace, and fair-tressed health. May you dispatch diseases and pain to the peaks of the mountains." Orphic Hymn 36 to Artemis (Translation: Athanassakis, A. N. & Wolkow, B. M.)

There are no confirmed holy days for Abnoba. This is unfortunate, but it also means that we can decide for ourselves when to celebrate. We can use the typical 'Wheel of the Year' of many pagan paths if we so choose. We can also look at the days that Diana and Artemis were celebrated and see if those will work for Abnoba. Finally, we can utilize the Coligny Calendar to determine the dates for our holidays. I employ a combination of methods in my practice and it seems so far that Abnoba has approved.

Coligny Calendar

There is evidence of a Gaulish calendar from Coligny, France. The calendar, frequently referred to as the Coligny Calendar, was found in 1897. It is a lunisolar calendar which means that it attempts to line the lunar months up with the solar year. It is set up with a five-year cycle of sixty-two months. Each month will have either 30 days, which are labeled MAT, or 29 days, which are labeled ANM. It is believed by some that these are abbreviations from the words *matti*, meaning 'good' and *anmatti*, meaning 'not good' (Widugeni, 2018. p. 98). In each cycle of 5 years there are 3 years with 12 months and 2 years that include 13 months. This gives two intercalary months to help align it with the solar year.

You will find that among the aspects of modern Gaulish Polytheism, the calendar remains one of the most hotly debated topics. The names of the months are available to us, as well as the previous information given. We also know that the year begins with the month of Samonios. The trouble is that no one is certain where the month of Samonios falls within the year. There are various schools of thought on the subject. Another area of contention is the start of the month. We can assume that it starts on a specific moon phase, but which phase is unknown. To get a working calendar you must decide where you think the month of Samonios should fall and what moon phase the month should begin on.

For the purposes of this book, I have decided to refer to the calendar dates of my friends at Nouiogalatis.org. They have developed a great system that I agree with on many points. There is actually an app that has been developed for the Coligny Calendar and their calendar aligns perfectly with it. This calendar places the month of Samonios roughly towards the second half of May. Below I will list the Coligny month names with their respective, albeit rough, Gregorian months in parentheses that correspond to their vision of the calendar.

Samonios (May-June)
Dumannios (June-July)
Riuros (July-August)
Anagantios (August-September)

Ogronios (September-October)

Cutios (October-November)

Giamonios (November-December)

Simiuisonna (December-January)

Equos (January-February)

Elembiuos (February-March)

Edrinios (March-April)

Cantlos (April-May)

They begin the months on the first quarter moon as this is a fairly easy moon phase to recognize. The two intercalary months are called Quimonios and Rantaranos. If you wish to learn more, I highly recommend the Nouiogalatis.org website as it is very informative.

I recently began celebrating my festivals according to this calendar to keep it as authentically Gaulish as I can. As such, I will offer those approximate dates for your use. However, I know many prefer the common Gregorian Calendar so I will also offer alternative dates that you could celebrate on. I must admit that I am a creature of habit. I was quite used to the Gregorian Calendar and since so much of my life is centered around it that was when I typically set my holy days to. However, with a little patience, learning the Coligny Calendar has been a much easier transition than I anticipated.

Comparative Method

As stated elsewhere, I am a Gaulish Polytheist, but I am also slightly influenced by Greco-Roman and even Germanic elements. Due to this, the comparative method does inform my practice to some extent. That being said, I thought I would start by using this method. I will examine holy days for other goddesses and use them to create a unique holiday for Abnoba. We will begin by looking at Diana as she is probably the goddess most similar to Abnoba and find a time to coincide with her great festival. From there, we will look at the festivals that are held in honor or Artemis and find an approximate date using the Coligny Calendar to celebrate Abnoba. Please note that we will be attempting to align a few very different calendars. This means the dates will be highly approximated. Additionally, it should be noted that in practice these Gaulish dates typically have other deities being honored at any given festival, but I will only be highlighting ways to honor Abnoba at these festivals. Again, I recommend Nouiogalatis.org if you are interested in learning other ways to celebrate on these dates. Many of the names for the holy days I celebrate are directly borrowed from them. Finally, I will offer a total of eight festivals on the Coligny Calendar to honor Abnoba. Feel free to celebrate on as many or as few of these days that you desire. My only intention is to give you several options to celebrate Abnoba throughout the year.

Diana's Sacred Day

In the Roman Empire the Nemoralia served as the most sacred day dedicated to Diana. This name can be translated as the 'Festival of Torches'. It was given this name due to worshippers gathering by torch and candlelight at Lake Nemi. The sanctuary of Diana at Lake Nemi is the original site of the festivities. The festival was initially celebrated on either the full moon of August, or on the 13th of that month, in which case it would end on the 15th. This was a time when Diana was honored in all of her aspects. According to the group Nova Roma, an organization dedicated to the modern practice of Roman Religion, Diana was celebrated at this time as the 'Lady of the Wilds', Mistress of the Beasts', 'Goddess of the Moon', 'Guardian of the Oak', 'Friend of the Nymph', 'Grand Midwife', and the 'Protector of Maidens'.

Additional information from Nova Roma mentions that there was a special ritual for washing the participants hair before placing flowers in it. In addition, dogs were also decorated with flowers. Prayers and wishes were written on ribbons and tied to trees. Common sacrifices included fruits, small sculptures of stags, or sculptures of mothers and children. For healing, bread or clay was used to shape into the body part where the ailment was located, and subsequently offered to Diana. Additionally, there was no hunting or killing of any animal during the time of this festival. During Nemoralia slaves and women were free from their obligations and were seen as equal to free men.

This gives us a few options to choose from for a celebration of Abnoba. It could be held on the full moon of August. As it is a three-day festival you could celebrate the day before the full moon, the day of, and the day after. Likewise, you could celebrate on the 13th, 14th, and 15th as they also held the Nemoralia on those dates. Finally, this date falls close to the Irish festival of Lughnasa which is also a common pagan holy day in the Wheel of the Year. So, if you choose you could honor Abnoba on this date. Any of these options would work. It is really only a choice that you can decide on. In our modern world with our busy schedules, it is actually common practice to celebrate these days on the closest weekend to the date of your choosing.

I choose to celebrate this day so that it coincides with Cintumessus which means 'First Harvest'. This day falls two first quarter moons after the summer solstice. It will vary from year to year which month this falls in, but it is either Anagantios or Riuros. I typically celebrate Abnoba as Dêuâ Sterî, the 'Goddess of the Homestead' during this festival. When I discovered Nemoralia was so close to this date it just felt right to me.

The information that we have of the Nemoralia also offers us ideas on how we can celebrate. Various offerings can be made to Abnoba in the form of fruit and baked goods. If you have an ailment, maybe bake the bread in the shape of the afflicted body part and offer a portion to Abnoba in the guise of Dêuâ Iaccî, or the 'Goddess of Health'. The idea of baking for a festival this time of year is actually quite common in many pagan paths. Perhaps you could bake a loaf in the shape of a deer or a dog. I would not worry about it looking perfect as your intention is the most important aspect. You could even simply make offerings of flowers. As plants are sacred to Abnoba I find that this is quite fitting.

Festivals of Artemis

Now I will shift the focus to the Greek Artemis. Artemis was quite popular in Ancient Greece and had a number of celebrations. We do not have a ton of information available about all of them, but we do have enough to give us some ideas.

Elaphebolia

Elaphebolia was celebrated on the 6th day of Elaphebolion. The Ancient Greek month of Elaphebolion is roughly equivalent to late March and early April of the Gregorian Calendar. The month would begin on the new moon. The festival would take place six days after the new moon. The day was particularly sacred to Artemis Elaphebolos meaning Artemis the 'Deer Slayer'. I put a slight spin on this aspect and honor Her as Abnoba Caruogenetâ, or the 'Deer Maiden'. According to the group Hellenion, an organization dedicated to the practice of Hellenic Polytheism, Artemis was offered *elaphoi,* or stags, which were stag-shaped cakes made of dough, honey and sesame seeds.

We are once again given a few options to celebrate. You could use the same date as the historical Elaphebolia. You could also choose the spring equinox to celebrate, or even the first full moon following the spring equinox. However, in a more Gaulish context you can celebrate a few days after the new moon closest to the vernal equinox. This will either be the 25th of Edrinios or the 25th of Elembiuos. This coincides with Uisonnalitus which means 'Spring Feast'. We are given another holy day that you could offer baked goods to Abnoba. As a goddess of homesteading, baking seems befitting to Abnoba. She always seems to approve of these offerings.

Mounykhia

Mounykhia is an ancient festival of the Athenians in honor of Artemis Mounykhia. This aspect of Artemis was sacred to the port in Attica. The festivities were held on the 16th day of the Ancient Greek month of Mounykhion, or sixteen days after the new moon of April. This is typically the beginning of Gregorian May. According to Hellenion the festival was occasionally celebrated the night of a full moon if the 16th day did not have a full moon. This is supposedly due to the Lunar aspect of Artemis being celebrated at this festival. She was also honored at this time as Potnia Theron, 'Mistress of the Animals'. It was common to sacrifice she-goats to Artemis during the event. In addition, a procession of young girls would walk to Artemis' temple with round cakes called *amphiphontes*, or 'shining all around'. These were made to symbolize the full moon.

For this sacred day I honor Abnoba as Riganâ Milon, 'Queen of Animals' and Argantoleucâ, the 'Silver Light'. You could celebrate this day on the 1st of May. Though you could just as easily choose the full moon of April or May closest to the first. The 1st of May coincides with the Irish Bealtaine so you could even choose that date. Finally, from a more Gaulish perspective, you could celebrate on Cintusamos, which means 'Start of Summer'. This festival falls two first quarter moons before the summer solstice. The corresponding month would be the 1st of either Samonios, Cantlos, or Quimonios. For my region this is a perfect day to celebrate spring. Where I am from the flowers have started to bloom and you can definitely feel the season is in bloom as well. We are, once again, presented with a holy day that baked goods can be offered. I will go into other offerings in the following chapter, but baked goods always make a superb offering.

Thargelia

Thargelia was another Athenian festival. It was held in honor of Apollo and Artemis' birthdays. As such, it is specific to them and would not necessarily translate into a festival for Abnoba. I mention it because it could give you the idea to choose a day and celebrate the birth of Abnoba. Interestingly, Arrian mentions that a hunter goddess of the Celts was honored with the first-fruits of the hunt on the birthday of the goddess (Green, 1992, p. 62). There is the slight possibility that the goddess discussed could have been Abnoba. If not, it still offers more precedence for having such a festival. Apollo and Artemis' birthday were celebrated on the 6th and 7th day of the month of Thargelion. The month of Thargelion is roughly equivalent to late May and early June in the Gregorian Calendar. However, you could celebrate any day that you choose. The Thargelia was primarily an agricultural event where the first fruits were offered to the gods. This could provide you with some inspiration to try and coincide the festival with a natural cycle of nature that is important to you.

Kharisteria

This was an ancient Athenian festival held to honor Artemis for the victory of Athens at Marathon against the Persians. The festival takes place on the 6th day of the month of Boidromion. This is equivalent to late September and early October in the Gregorian Calendar. The name Kharisteria means 'Thanksgiving'. In ancient times 500 goats were offered to Artemis to give her thanks. I celebrate this day as Îuos Bratous, or 'Festival of Thanks'. This is held two or three days after the new moon closest to the autumnal equinox. Typically, this falls on the 25th of either Anagantios or Ogronios.

Sacred Day of the 6th

It was common practice for the Athenians to celebrate certain deities every month on specific days. You may have noticed that many of the Greek times of celebration for Artemis were celebrated on the 6ᵗʰ of their respective months. This is because the number six was sacred to Artemis. So Artemis was honored every month six days after the new moon. Occasionally she was apparently celebrated on the 16ᵗʰ as well. In my research I could not find any specific practices tied to these days. However, maybe there is a number that is important to you and that you feel is connected to Abnoba in some way. Feel free to honor Her every month on that particular day.

Sacred Month

In addition to these sacred days Artemis was also given an entire month. The month of Artemisios was a part of the ancient Macedonian Calendar. This was roughly equivalent to late April and early May of the Gregorian Calendar. There is no reason you cannot honor Abnoba all month long during a time of your choosing if you desire. I offer to Abnoba on a near daily basis as it is. The majority of my spiritual calendar consists of holy days dedicated to Her and I try to make an offering at the full moon each month. As it stands, I do not personally have a month dedicated to Her as She already serves in such a large manner in my life already.

Brauronia

One other festival is Brauronia. This celebrated Artemis Braironia, and took place every four to five years in Brauron. According to Hellenion, a procession of girls and boys would walk to the sanctuary of Artemis. Once there they would sacrifice a goat to Her. Then they would perform the Arkteia, or the 'bear dance'. This was considered a rite of passage, particularly for girls as it consecrated virgins before they could marry. While this was an important festival and it certainly sounds interesting, it is not one that I actively participate in or celebrate. That is not to say that Abnoba would not respond to it, and that you could not create your own version of the festival with similar elements.

Perhaps you could honor Her as Caruogenetâ at this time. There are more holy days celebrating Artemis on the Greek calendars. However, several either do not really apply to Abnoba, or we do not have very much information or dates for them. Between the Roman Nemoralia and the Greek festivals we are given several interesting dates to celebrate. There are additional dates that I celebrate as well. I will discuss these below.

Reconstructed Holy Days

In my sacred calendar, I celebrate any number of gods and goddesses. Abnoba has increasingly taken center stage during the majority of my holy days. As such, I celebrate Her at nearly every festival that I honor the Gaulish Deuoi. This turns out to somewhat coincide with the 'Wheel of the Year,' but with a Gaulish flair. I find that this schedule of holidays lines up fairly well with the natural cycles where I live. Put simply, it makes sense to celebrate on these dates. What follows are the remaining four festivals and why I celebrate them.

Adbiuos

The name of this holiday comes from the Gaulish word meaning 'to life, quickening'. Adbiuos takes place two first quarter moons after the winter solstice. This falls on the 1st of either Equos or Elembiuos. This is approximately near the 1st of February, coinciding with the Irish and Pagan holiday of Imbolc. This is the pre-spring holiday. As such, it is the time when I begin my spring cleaning. As someone who struggles with mental health issues, cleaning and organizing is vitally important to my state of mind. I always tell myself *messy house, messy mind*. This also corresponds to the time of year when deer in my area shed their antlers. I look at this as emblematic for myself. As the deer shed their antlers, I shed anything old and unwanted that I may have. I offer my work up as an offering to Abnoba Dêuâ Sterî and Caruogenetâ in addition to more traditional offerings.

Samolitus

Samolitus translates to 'Summer Festival'. This takes place on the first quarter moon before the summer solstice which falls on the 1st of either Dumannios or Samonios. You could also celebrate on the summer solstice as this is the common pagan holy day of Midsummer, or Litha. This time of year, I am busy doing lots of work in the yard and gardens. As Abnoba is connected to nature I feel like this is a great way to honor Her. This is also the time of year where deer gather in pastures to graze on the abundant plant life. Again, this seems like a meaningful comparison to make. We like to cook out on this day and have a nice summertime feast to enjoy this bountiful season. On this day I also try to make it a goal to get out and see one of the beautiful parks in my local area. A portion of my meal is usually offered to Abnoba along with other seasonal items. At this festival Abnoba is honored as Caruogenetâ once again.

Îuos Antumnî

Îuos Antumnî means the 'Otherworld Festival' and is a time to honor the ancestors. This roughly corresponds to the Irish and Pagan Samhain. I celebrate two first quarter moons before the winter solstice. This is usually the 1st of Giamonios, but can also be the 1st of either Cutios or Rantaranos. I honor Abnoba as Dêuâ Antî, or the 'Goddess of Boundaries'. This aspect is very close to my heart. It is in this role that I had one of my most profound religious experiences. It was a highly personal experience that involved the death of my grandmother. As previously referenced, I did not know until much later that it was Abnoba guiding me that night. When I made the connection to Abnoba I felt this instant pull in my heart and I knew it to be Her. Needless to say, this is a very important holy day. The day is spent in reverence for my ancestors, be they blood, marriage, or even spiritual ancestors, and making offerings to them.

Giamolitus

Giamolitus is the 'Winter Festival' and it is spent honoring Abnoba as Dêuâ Allatês, 'Goddess of the Wilds'. This typically falls on the full moon closest to the winter solstice. This will be on either the 9th of Giamonios or Simiuisonna. This, of course, aligns it very closely with the common holy days of Yule, or Midwinter. This is the most desolate time of year for many. It is because of this that I think it fits in quite nicely with the theme of the unknown wilderness and Abnoba as Dêuâ Allatês.

Full Calendar

From this we can now present eight seasonal festivals to celebrate Abnoba in various aspects. Below I have placed them in list form. This includes the accompanying moon phases for those that wish to celebrate them by using the form of the Coligny Calendar that has been presented here.

Cintusamos – Two First Quarter Moons before the Summer Solstice

Samolitus – First Quarter Moon before the Summer Solstice

Cintumessus – Two First Quarter Moons after the Summer Solstice

Îuos Bratous – Few Days after the New Moon closest to the Autumnal Equinox

Îuos Antumnî – Two First Quarter Moons before the Winter Solstice

Giamolitus – Full Moon closest to the Winter Solstice

Adbiuos – Two First Quarter Moons after the Winter Solstice

Uisonnalitus – Few Days after the New Moon closest to the Vernal Equinox

Conclusion

The methods I used to create a working set of festivals may not be for everyone. It is my hope that this gives you at least a few ideas to celebrate and honor Abnoba in your own way. Even if you are not a big fan of the days that I chose, I hope that you can put your own spin on them. The main point is to honor and celebrate Abnoba for the gifts that She can offer to you. Now that you have some ideas for festival dates, we can turn our focus to creating sacred spaces and finding suitable offerings in the next chapter.

Chapter 6

Altars and Offerings

"Hear me, O revered goddess, O many-named divinity, O sight sweet to women in labor, you offer them aid in travail. You save women, and you alone love children, O Kindly goddess of swift birth, ever helpful to young women, O Prothyraia. You hold the keys, you are accessible to all, O mistress, gracious and fond of nurture, you have power in every house, and you delight in festivities. You loosen girdles, and thought invisible you are seen in every deed, you share pain, you rejoice in every birth, O Eileithyia, you free from pain those in terrible distress. Upon you alone pregnant women call, O comforter of souls, and in you alone there is relief from pains of labor. Artemis, Eileithyia, reverend Prothyraia, hear, O blessed one, help me and grant offspring; save me, savior of all, for it is in your nature to do so." Orphic Hymn 2 to Prothyraia (Artemis) (Translation: Athanassakis, A. N. & Wolkow, B. M.)

Sacred Space

It is believed that the ancient Gauls did not practice their religion in temples until the Romans came along. Before that we know that they had *nemetons*, meaning a 'sanctuary, sacred wood' (Delamarre, 2003, p. 17). They would also frequently honor certain gods, particularly those associated with healing, at an *andounna*, or 'water from below, source; spring source' (Delamarre, 2003, p. 2). In addition, the andounna could also be a pit for placing offerings (Widugeni, 2018, p. 77). While having a sacred space like this is ideal, it is unfortunately out of reach for most of us. Alternatively, our homes can serve as sacred spaces. Unless you have a spot out in nature where you feel you can commune with deity better, in which case, by all means have at it!

As far as a daily practice goes it is best to have an altar. A term among some modern Gaulish Polytheists for altar is the word *aidu*. This actually means something along the lines of sacrificial fire. As a fire is a central element to our altars this does make sense. Building an altar to commune with the divine is great to do if you can. A sacred space can make all the difference. Ideally this would have centered on the hearth. Most homes today no longer have a hearth, but in the past, this was the sacred center of the home. One can still construct a sacred space. A side table, bookshelf, many things can be used as an altar. The typical altar will face east, the direction of the rising sun. However, this is not a requirement.

What do you put on your Altar?

Your altar can consist of many things. In a Gaulish context you should probably have at least a candle, which serves as the sacred fire, and an offering dish. If you can, a burner for incense is good to have as well. After that the only limit is your imagination. I like to change my altar up between the holy days. Your altar and offerings will form a significant part of your devotional practice. The altar provides us with a sacred space to work with Abnoba. It is a way to really hone our focus to improve the quality of our worship. Offerings serve to show our devotion to a particular deity or spirit. It is a part of the gifting cycle. The deity, in our case Abnoba, provides us with support and help on our path and in return we offer Her gifts. It is a reciprocal relationship.

My altar, at least my primary one as I have a few, is predominantly dedicated to Abnoba. If you are fortunate enough to have the space then an image or something representative of the deity can really help focus energy and attention to them. I try to include a few things to represent Abnoba, but I also try to avoid clutter. That being said, I have seen altars that are filled with items and I still find them incredibly beautiful. There truly are no limits. I currently have a statue that I found used to represent Abnoba, two small candles, two offering dishes (one for liquid offerings and one for dry offerings) and an incense burner.

One of my offering dishes is a bowl that I offer water in. This serves as a mock andounna on my altar as water was sacred to Abnoba. Other items I like to change seasonally. I place certain flowers on my altar in the spring and summer. In the autumn I may trade those out for crisp fallen leaves and acorns. You may also include a mortar and pestle on your altar if you make your own incense or herbal poultices. Various traditions have certain requirements for altars, and if you belong to one of them feel free to include those items as well.

Do you need an Altar?

One of the first questions you may ask yourself is do you need to have an altar. The short answer is no, you are not required to have an altar. You are not bound to do anything that you do not desire to do. If you want my opinion on what you should do then I say, yes, if you can get one.

The main point of an altar, for myself, is to have a dedicated sacred space in my home. A place where I can go at any time and turn off this world and engage with Abnoba in the *Otherworld*. Having an altar really helps you shift your mind to the sacred and away from the profane.

Unfortunately, we are not all fortunate enough to have the space to have an altar. Or maybe your living situations preclude you from being 'out' about your faith. In my experience the deities understand these issues so please do not be hard on yourself. If this does include you, I may have a solution for you below.

Setting up your Altar

To begin, an altar can be a lot of different things to a lot of different people. At minimum I suggest a candle, a way to deliver an offering such as a small plate or bowl, and some representation of Abnoba, or any other deity that you feel called to. This can be anything that connects you to Her. Maybe you have found a stone that feels special. As a goddess of nature, I find that found objects do resonate well with Abnoba.

If space or location are issues for you then you may consider a small portable altar. This is also beneficial if you are not out to others about your spiritual path. A portable altar offers mobility so you can locate a private spot *somewhere* to make an offering. Just be sure you are not on private property. To create a portable altar simply find yourself a small tin. For instance, some candy and breath fresheners come in tins that are the perfect size for what you need. It only needs to be big enough to hold a tea light candle, matches or a lighter, and perhaps a small image or object you have found that can represent Abnoba. You can take this, as well as your offering, anywhere (again without trespassing) that you desire. I just ask that if you are outside, please be careful with the fire. It does not take much for a forest to go up in flames. This would be horrific on its own, but it certainly would not be taken well by Abnoba either.

If space and privacy are not an issue then I do recommend getting an altar. Any flat surface will do. A shelf, bookcase, nightstand or end table will all work great. Additionally, feel free to place other things on your altar that help you tap into the sacred. This can be a special stone you found or a picture of a recently deceased ancestor.

Altar Tools and Meaning

A lot can be said about what you should include on your altar, and you would be hard pressed to find two people who recommend the same things. I try to keep it fairly simple. The majority of my altar items represent the realms, or worlds, of Gaulish Polytheism.

The three realms are a common theme in a lot of Indo-

European mythologies. The Gaulish system views the three realms as: *Albios*, *Dumnos* and *Bitus*. Albios is the sky, home of the celestial deities (Widugeni, 2018, p. 26). Another term for sky is *Nemos*, though this may refer specifically to the physical sky. Dumnos, or Dubnos, is the deep, home of chthonic deities and some spirits of the dead (Widugeni, 2018, p. 27). Dumnos is also home to chthonic beings and ancestors. Another word for Dumnos is *Mori*, although this word is more specifically related to the sea. Bitus is this world, the realm of humanity (Widugeni, 2018, p. 26). This is also the home of plants, animals and some other earth-bound spirits as well.

It is not a requirement for you to have representation of the three realms on your altar. If you decide that you would like to, you can use incense to represent the celestial realm of Albios. A bowl of water can represent the chthonic realm of Dumnos. You can use salt or a stone to represent this world, Bitus. I personally consider the altar itself as representative of Bitus.

Some people may opt for altar items that represent the classical elements of earth, air, water, fire and spirit though this is not a part of Gaulish Polytheism. Your path may require fewer items, or a number of different items that you may wish to incorporate. This is a highly personal space. One that you will share with Abnoba, so make it a special and sacred place. I have included a few items below and explain the purpose of these objects in further detail.

Cauldron

In lieu of a bowl you can use a *pario*, which is the Gaulish word for cauldron (Delamarre, 2003, Pg. 19). The cauldron is representative of Dumnos and mori, the sea, or abyss. It is symbolic of the afterlife and the Otherworld. It is the home of our ancestors who have moved on. When working with the elements of Dumnos you can honor Abnoba as Dêuâ Antî, Goddess of Boundaries, as this role has otherworldly connections. The cauldron, if large enough, can be used in place of the offering dish if you choose. The cauldron that I have is made of bronze. Something to keep in mind, the cauldron that I use is actually rather large, as such I have to place mine on a shelf below my altar. I do not use it in all of my workings so this is convenient for me. You may wish to obtain a smaller one if you only plan to use it for small offerings, but it is not required.

Incense and Incense Holder

Incense is a cleansing tool. For our purposes it is a symbol of Albios and nemos, the sky, as its smoke carries our prayers to the heavens. Albios is the realm of the Gods and other celestial beings. The incense holder serves as a safe place to burn our incense so make sure that it is designed to do so. You can work with Abnoba in a couple of roles when trying to incorporate Albios into your workings. You could invoke Her as Argantoleucâ, or as Dêuâ Iaccî.

Candle

The candle is representative of the active element of fire. It is change, it is life, it is destruction. Fire lies within us, above us, and below us. It is a critical element to my altar, and as it is the sacrificial fire it should be the center of your altar as well. As the sacred flame also serves to represent the hearth you could invoke Abnoba as Dêuâ Sterî, Goddess of the Homestead. If you cannot have a lit candle for whatever reason there are a variety of battery powered candles that will work just as well.

Offering Dish

The offering dish is a sacred plate or bowl used to symbolically make your offering to Abnoba, or any other deity. Making offerings is critical in relationships with the divine as it enables you to participate in the reciprocal gifting cycle. As this is used for offerings, and not for burning, it may be made of any number of items. I use a small ceramic bowl.

On the Subject of Offerings

So far, I have made several references to offerings for Abnoba. I thought I would take this opportunity to dive a little bit deeper into this topic. Frequent questions that people ask include what items make suitable offerings? Some want to know what to do with said offerings, and how to dispose of the offering. We will tackle these questions here.

What Can You Offer?

Offerings will vary from person to person and from deity to deity. In this case we will discuss offerings specifically aimed for Abnoba. We will begin with my go-to offering; incense. Incense is a suitable offering to just about any god or goddess. This goes without saying that incense itself is an excellent way to help center yourself before beginning a ritual or prayer.

Another routine offering that I give to Abnoba is water. As a goddess intimately tied to rivers and water in general, I feel that this is a great offering. I do feel that rain water or water from a stream is best, but I know that is not always an option on a regular basis. Every morning I take my offering dish and place a bit of water in it. At night I will take it outside and pour it out.

Other suitable offerings include items such as pears, apples, blueberries or any other fruit you may wish to use. As a goddess of the forest and plants any tree or bush bearing fruit make excellent offerings. Leaves and herbs can be offered as can stones. Baked goods are very common offerings to Diana and Artemis so I feel these would work for Abnoba as well. She is a goddess of homesteading and I feel that baking is a part of that. You could make fresh baked bread or cookies in the shape of animals like dogs or deer. Store bought does work in a pinch, but I think she appreciates the extra effort of homemade. Honey and maple syrup could be offered. Additionally, apple cider is a good offering in lieu of alcohol. I do not personally drink, but some people do offer things like mead or wine to the gods and I cannot imagine Her rejecting it. Giving a portion of your meals is a common offering to any of the gods and Abnoba seems accepting of that as well.

Finally, you do not need to always offer objects. Our actions can be given as offerings as well. I mentioned earlier that I am a soap maker. Each time that I make soap it is a sacred process for me that I dedicate to Abnoba. As a goddess with connections to healing soap seems like an essential building block to good health. This could also tie in to Her homesteading role. On the subject of homesteading there are numerous activities you can participate in and dedicate your service to Abnoba. Recycling is a great thing to do for a variety of reasons. Composting, gardening and tending to your land are other meaningful gestures.

You can also donate your time by volunteering at charities and on various other projects. Donating your time to an animal rescue is a great offering. Another is participating in programs that benefit children. It is always dependent on the intent that you have. I try to do many things in my life with a lot of focused intent to make the actions appropriate offerings to Abnoba. Every meal that I make is an offering in itself; for good health is a way to show Abnoba I am doing my part. Every time I exercise is an offering to Abnoba. Every positive choice that I make to improve my health rather it be physical, mental, or spiritual is an offering.

Are you an artist, a writer, or a dancer? If you have any artistic talent at all then use your art as an offering. I think an artist is in all of us. It is just harder for some of us to realize what our exact talent is. Find a way that you can use your art as an offering. Choreograph a small dance. Paint a picture as an offering. Of course, if you are writing your own prayers that is an artistic offering as well. The only limit to offerings truly is your own imagination.

How to Dispose of Offerings?

This is a subject that many are divided on. Some people simply throw the offering in the trash the day after it is made or later on in the evening. I hate to waste food, and I do not feel that Abnoba is a fan of wasted food either. I know that making an offering should not be considered wasting, and perhaps that is a poor phrase to use. There will indeed be 'leftovers' once Abnoba is finished with the offering. The easiest way to avoid this is to simply compost the leftovers instead of just trashing them. This way they can play a vital role in the creation of new plant life as they are returned to the earth. In the same manner you can also bury the offering. Additionally, you can leave the offering outside and let nature run its course. If it is a drink, you can simply pour it out onto the ground.

There is an exception to this method. I am not an expert on indigenous tribes and I do not pretend to be. I do live in the United States. It is because of this that I will just say here that if you do as well it may not be appropriate for you to simply pour out offerings of alcohol onto the earth. I have seen conflicting opinions on this matter, but I avoid it. This just comes from my experience as a polytheist of privilege living on the former lands of Indigenous Americans. It is an easy thing not to do so I have always avoided this act.

Conclusion

I hope that this chapter gave you the confidence to set up your own sacred space. I think you will find it is very rewarding. If you were scared to make offerings, I hope that now you feel safe doing so. In all actuality I do not think there is much that you cannot use to make an offering. Abnoba seems appreciative of everything that I have offered to Her in the past. I am sure She will be equally as pleased with your offerings.

Chapter 7

Prayer and Meditation

"We belong to Diana, girls and chaste boys: chaste boys and girls, we sing Diana.
Diana Latonia, queenly Daughter of Zeus, birthed at the olive tree, we sing Diana.
Mountain mistress at the gates of sylvan green, secret glen, sounding stream, we sing Diana.
In childbirth, you are Juno Lucina, other times bold Trivia or the borrowed light of the moon: we sing Diana.
Dividing the year by menses you fill with good fruit the farmers' rustic lofts: we sing Diana.
Whatever name you choose, protect the children of Rome as you did in days of old: we sing Diana." The Poems of Catullus: 34 Diana's Song (Catullus, G. V., Uzzi, J. D., & Thomson, J. p. 63)

Reaching Out

When it comes to reaching out to the divine, we are left with a variety of options. This chapter will focus on ways for you to communicate with Abnoba, or any other deity you find has come into your life for that matter. Some of these methods will be as simple as saying a couple of words, and others will be slightly more advanced in their phrasing. Despite the difference in structure these methods should be available to any of us regardless of finances or any other mitigating factors. I have never believed that we need expensive materials and overly elaborate rituals to commune with deity. I find that Abnoba is particularly responsive whenever and however I reach out to Her.

Prayer

I have a very devotional practice. By this I mean that much of the work that I do involves devotional activities aimed at honoring Abnoba and other spirits. As such a large part of me honoring the deities and spirits include both prayer and ritual. I have honored a fairly large number of deities in my time and prayer is by far the easiest, and perhaps the most intimate, step that we can take to communicate with the divine. It is prayer that led me to have the relationship with Abnoba that I do. Speaking to Her on a regular basis has served to deepen our bond.

Prayer can be very simple and you can just say what you feel in the moment. Prayer can also be highly stylized and take hours, or more, to write. It depends on what you feel comfortable with and what the deity responds to. I find with Abnoba that I typically use prayers that I have already written, but I did not spend hours writing them. Occasionally, I will simply speak from the heart to offer Her gratitude for Her blessings, but more often than not I have set prayers that I recite. If you are not comfortable writing your own prayers then try modifying prayers that someone else has written.

Hourly Prayer

Monastic elements play a critical part in my spiritual life. It is because of this that I allot certain times of the day to solely focus on my prayers. This is, of course, much easier said than done for many of us. It has taken a great amount of time and dedication to be sure that I stick to these set prayer times.

Yes, I am not perfect and there are days when I have shifted the time. The point is to try. The more that I do stick to my specified times, the more orderly the rest of my day seems to go. Are you required to do this? Absolutely not! Life gets in the way, emergencies happen, and other things take priority. I just feel it is a good practice to have something to strive towards. It truly has made a difference to my practice, and in my life.

Many different religious paths ask various levels of dedication. Some of them are quite demanding and far out of the scope of what I could hope, or want, to achieve. We will not get into all of those paths here as there are far better sources for that subject than I. However, it is my personal objective to say three separate prayers at specified times of the day. These are relatively short and easy to remember as we shall discuss soon. First, a bit about the types of prayers.

Types of Prayer

Depending on who you ask, there can be numerous types of prayers. In this section we will primarily focus on two very broad categories of prayer: prayers of petition and prayers of praise. These two types of prayer are fairly self-explanatory. We will discuss both of these types of prayers below. Keep in mind that there are more than just these two types, and that even these types of prayer can be subdivided further.

Prayers of Praise

A prayer of praise is exactly what it sounds like. This is a type of prayer where praise is given to the deity in question. This can be as simple as a thank you for gifts that they have given, or just praise to a deity for being there in your life.

On a typical day I offer several prayers of praise to Abnoba. I begin with a rising prayer upon waking up. Then before I eat dinner, I will offer a prayer of thanksgiving. Finally, before bed I will offer an evening prayer. These are all three kept relatively short to be easy to remember. I am not my best at speaking off the cuff so I prefer to have something written beforehand. If you do not like to be so formal just speak straight from your heart. I will display my prayers here to offer some inspiration, but please keep in mind the power of writing your own.

This first prayer is my rising prayer. I say it each morning once I have woken up. This prayer is an excellent way to start your day and offer your work of the day to Abnoba. I honor three aspects of Abnoba in this prayer. I pray to Her as a goddess of health for the hope of good health each day. I pray to Her as a goddess of boundaries as it can represent my day's journey. Finally, I honor Her as a goddess of the wilds to represent the unknown that the day will bring. You will see that I occasionally rely on rhymes to help with memorization, but I am not a fanatic on following any specific structure.

Rising Prayer
Abnoba, Dêuâ Iaccî
I awaken on this day
Thankful for good health
Your guidance lights the way
Abnoba, Dêuâ Antî
I rise up on this day
I explore the boundaries
Holding negativity at bay
Abnoba, Dêuâ Allatês
I march out on this day
I journey into the wilds
In your name I pray

This second prayer is what most people would refer to as a prayer of thanksgiving. This is offered before my largest meal of the day. It is a simple thanks for the bounty that Abnoba has provided.

Prayer of Thanksgiving
Abnoba, hear my praise
For this meal you have given
For this drink I have risen
Because Your gifts keep me driven
I send You praise every day, and in every way

This third prayer is my evening prayer. I will say this prayer before my husband and I go to bed and watch a little television at night. This prayer is utilized as a way to ask for pleasant dreams. I have always had sleep issues, both insomnia and narcolepsy, so I understand that sleep is a very important part of our overall well being. As Abnoba oversees the nighttime, in Her role as a goddess of the Moon, I think that this really resonates with Her.

Evening Prayer
Abnoba Argantoleucâ
I ask you for restful sleep
Great Goddess of the streams
I wish for visions deep
Your radiant light it gleams
My devotion you may keep
I pray for sweet dreams

As you can see each of these prayers are fairly simple. You are free to use these prayers whenever you like. However, I will again encourage you to try and write your own. At the very least, tweak the ones that I have provided to better suit your spiritual needs. There really are no rules to writing a prayer. You just need to speak sincerely from the heart.

There is one more devotional thing that I do daily. It is a very short prayer where I make an offering of either incense or water. I think of these as a great option for any deity, and for just about any occasion. I simply say:

Abnoba, Dêuâ Allatês, I offer you this incense.
I ask for your continued guidance and support.
I praise you and I go in peace.

This is short, simple, and to the point. It is just a great way to show Abnoba my gratitude on a daily basis. I usually do this devotional shortly before my evening prayer. However, due to schedule conflicts I have recently switched to doing this prayer earlier in the day.

Prayers of Petition

A prayer of petition is one of which you are probably most familiar. This is a prayer where you are asking for something. This can be anything. You could ask for spiritual guidance or even some form of monetary gain, and everything in between.

I think the key to making prayers of petition appropriate is to never look at the divine as your personal wish granting figures. That is not why they exist. They deserve our most sincere reverence. I would also avoid using prayers of petition for your first interaction with Abnoba. This is why I mentioned prayers of praise first. Build up to asking for something, and do not make the granting of said prayer the sole reason for your interaction.

I believe prayers of petition should be part of a reciprocal relationship. I make offerings and give praise on a routine basis. This makes the act of petitioning less presumptuous towards Abnoba. I still do not expect every prayer to come true, but if I focus my intent and ask Her for help then my chances are far greater than doing nothing.

It is additionally important to remember that these types of prayers need to be kept in line with reality. I could pray all day and every day for a million dollars, but unless I am actively doing something that could bring about that kind of change in my life it will not happen.

An example of a prayer of petition that Abnoba may help with is for granting good health or healing for a sick friend. For instance, you could say something as simple as:

Abnoba, Dêuâ Iaccî, please bless my friend
with good health and a quick recovery.
I praise you and I go in peace.

This is short and to the point. Try and really focus your intention on the request. If you like you can even make a small offering.

Additionally, to further things along with your sick friend, think of things *you* can do to help. Can the friend use some freshly made soup? Do they need help running an errand or two? These gestures show Abnoba how important this matter is to you and really center your mind on what you desire. This also serves to allow Abnoba to work through you, and helps to fuel the prayer. Prayer is not just a means of asking for whatever you desire and wishing it into existence. The effort that you put in will directly affect the outcome of any given prayer.

Invocation

An invocation is actually very similar to a prayer. The primary difference is you are summoning a deity for their spiritual presence. When you pray you are typically sending it out to their realm, whereas an invocation you are seeking their presence in our realm. For instance, when you are making an offering to Abnoba, you need Her to be present to accept your gift. So, an invocation is much more common in a ritual, and they are a bit more formal. Once again, this particular invocation calls Abnoba as a goddess of health. You could easily change a few things around to invoke another aspect of Abnoba.

I invoke Abnoba
Dêuâ Iaccî
I ask for blessings of health and healing
I give you this offering
Abnoba, your name I praise
I thank you

Meditation

In the previous section I discussed ways in which you can begin to reach out to Abnoba. We will continue with that theme, but

I feel that meditation is a great way for Abnoba to reach out to you. Proper meditation really requires a suspension of the mind that you may not access during prayer or just speaking out to Her.

That is not to say that you cannot experience Abnoba during prayer. In fact, over time you should always feel something when engaging with Her. Meditation just really opens the channels of communication to a whole new level. In this section we will dive into guided meditation and then the method of dream incubation.

Please note, when I say you should always feel something when praying, I do not mean that you should feel this magical divine moment whenever you pray. Some of us go our whole lives and never experience a moment like that. So please never let that discourage you. I just mean that after some time spent in prayer you begin to sense the prayer has been received. The deities are always listening whether they let us know or not.

Meditation Technique

A lot of people get intimidated by meditation, but with a little practice, and a lot of patience, you should be able to succeed. Meditation can be as simple as taking a nice calming walk where you clear your mind and open yourself up to actually listen to the deities. That is meditation in one of its simplest forms and one that I regularly employ. The method for meditating that I will describe below is a little more detailed, but still relatively simple.

I recommend listening to tracks of drumming while trying to meditate. Listening to repetitive drumming can lead to therapeutic effects especially if it is included with a guided meditation. Try and find one that is fifteen minutes long as studies show this is the amount of time it takes to reach maximum therapeutic benefits (Gingras, Pohler, & Fitch, 2014). There are several drumming sessions like this that you can find with a quick search online.

Find yourself a quiet place where you will not be disturbed. I like to meditate in front of my altar. Light a candle or some incense. Do whatever you need to do to help you relax and get into the right state of mind. Make sure you are sitting in a comfortable position as you will be sitting here for some time.

There are a few ways you can do this. The first is probably the hardest. You will read the following guided meditation and try to remember it, and then replay it in your mind as you walk through it. The second method is having a friend read the mediation for you while you walk through it. Finally, you can record yourself reciting the meditation and play it back while you walk through the meditation. This is my preferred method.

Begin by closing your eyes and taking several slow deep breaths in and out. Connect to the ground below you as you become centered.

Your surroundings begin to dissipate and you find yourself near the edge of a rolling meadow in front of a thick and dark forest. The air is fresh and slightly warm on your skin. It is a beautiful spring day. Bright and fragrant flowers accent the green field. You can smell just a hint of morning dew still fresh in the air. You hear a light breeze brushing over the meadow, and through the forest in front of you. In the distance, you hear birds singing their songs.

You feel called to the woodland; beckoned by some unknown force. As you slowly approach the woods you notice a trail that passes between two giant old oak trees that leads into the forest. You head steadily between them. Your feet transition from walking on a soft bed of grass to the crunch of smaller vegetation, leaves, and small broken twigs. You continue on this path for a bit taking in all that surrounds you in this forest.

Up ahead on the path there is a clearing in the woods. The sun's rays are shining toward the opening, illuminating it. You notice a

figure growing ever larger with each new step. The figure is luminous,
but you can't quite make it out. With each new step the figure becomes
more and more visible. You can finally see the figure is a beautiful
woman. You begin to make out Her image. This is Abnoba. What do
you see? What does she look like? Take in all the glorious details.

You notice the woman is seated on a large stone at the center of
the clearing. She welcomes you forward to sit next to her. You have
a seat and the two of you bask in the sunlight shimmering through
the opening of the clearing. She has so much knowledge, so much
experience, and so much guidance to impart to you. You ask her a
question you are longing to know the answer to. She speaks clearly and
answers your questions.

When you are ready you say goodbye, graciously extend your
gratitude to Her, and rise to leave. You head back the same way that
you came. You walk away from the clearing and into the darkened
forest. You follow the path back through the woods and out through
the two giant old oaks trees. As you leave the woods you are back in
the rolling meadow again. You casually make your way until you reach
your starting point.

Slowly and carefully come back to your present situation. Take a
moment to collect yourself before rising.

Get a pen or pencil and begin writing down your experience.
Write down every word that Abnoba spoke to you and every
detail that you can recall.

I hope that this is a helpful exercise for you. It has personally
worked for me a few times. I find if you are not successful to
keep practicing and eventually most people should be able to
have more success over time. Remember, the key to successful
meditation is patience and practice. Meditation will not always
click right away. Do not let that discourage you from trying.
Keep at it and each time you will get a little better than the last.
Personally, I have a very fast paced mind. To really 'turn-off' my
over-analyzing mind and get into the right state to meditate,

and visualize, still takes a lot of focus for me after all of these years.

Dream Incubation

While meditation is one great way to talk to Abnoba I find that dreams are another great tool to experience Her. Between the two, dreams are much harder to control than mediation. At least for most of us they are. Sometimes I am lucky enough to have a dream about Abnoba without assistance, but this is rare. Again, do not get discouraged. There is a method that helps me to better manage my dreams, and it is called dream incubation.

To practice dream incubation, you begin by simply planting a seed in your mind. This can be about a problem you are facing or an individual you are hoping to help. Essentially, whatever your heart desires you need to focus on it before falling asleep. Just as in meditation, it takes time, patience, and practice to achieve your desired goal, but the point is to find a solution, get an answer, or simply talk to Abnoba through your dreams. Sometimes our sleeping mind can come up with solutions when our waking mind cannot.

One of the harder parts of dream incubation is holding onto the image in your mind. Our minds, at least mine, tend to wander quite easily when trying to sleep. Perhaps place an object next to your bedside that is representative of your desired goal. Look at it before you turn off the lights. A picture would work if you want to dream about a specific person. Even an object that reminds you of someone or something can work.

Another thing to keep in mind is that when you wake up, do not jump right out of bed, and try to avoid distractions. This will commonly lead to you forgetting some of your dreams (Barrett, 2010). Lie there, and try to remember your dream. If you cannot then try and see how you feel. What kinds of emotions do you have? Keep a notebook or journal next to your bed and write down every detail that you can remember.

Finally, you must learn to discern what is truly Abnoba talking to you, and what is your subconscious mind talking to you. This will not come easily. It will take serious work to determine if what you dreamed was actually you reinforcing the answer that you already desire, or if you have indeed gathered divine insight.

Learning to understand what your inner voice sounds like can be a great help. If the answer you found is too good to be true, then the chances are good that it is. This does not necessarily mean that this solution is incorrect. It just means that it needs more scrutiny. Take what you learned and try your hand at a divination method of your choosing to seek further answers.

Dream incubation is a great skill that you can utilize in your work with Abnoba. Be it physical problems, mental health issues, or matters of the soul, we can seek Her support. It is a difficult practice, but with hard work, and support from Abnoba, one may just be able to achieve their goals.

Conclusion

It is my hope that this chapter served as a good primer on what you need to look for when encountering Abnoba. Open and honest communication, as with most relationships, is the key to strengthen this bond. Maybe you have been contacted by a different deity and not Abnoba. The same general rules apply to them as well. Start talking. Make an offering. See if you hear back from whoever is trying to reach out to you. If all goes well and you want to continue to grow this relationship maybe it is time to set up an altar. You will know when the time is right. For those that have formed a relationship with Abnoba, and you seek to start a more dedicated path with Her, the next chapter will be of great interest. Next, we will examine the steps of a dedication ritual.

Chapter 8

Dedication Ritual

"Goddess, queen of the woodlands – for thy countenance and honourable bearing proclaim thee of no mortal birth – thou who beneath this fiery vault art blest in needing not to search for water, succour a neighbouring people; whether the Wielder of the Bow or Latona's daughter hath set thee in the bridal-chamber from her chaste company, or whether it be no lowly passion but one from on high doth make thee fruitful – for the ruler of the gods himself is no stranger to Argive bowers – look upon our distressed ranks. Us hath the resolve to destroy guilty Thebes with the sword brought hither, but the unwarlike doom of cruel drought doth bow our spirits and drain our exhausted strength. Help thou our failing fortunes, whether thou hast some turbid river or a stagnant marsh; nought is to be held shameful, nought too mean in such a pass as ours. Thee now in place of the Winds and rainy Jupiter do we supplicate, do thou restore our ebbing might and fill again our spiritless hearts; so may thy charge grow under suspicious stars! Only let Jupiter grant us to return, what high-piled booty of war shalt thou be given! With the blood of numerous herds of Dirce will I recompense thee, O goddess, and a mighty altar shall mark this grove." Statius Thebaid IV 746-764 (Translation Mozley, J. H.)

Performing rituals does not need to be complex. The simple act of lighting a candle, saying a prayer, and making an offering is a ritual itself. It really does not need to go any further than that. However, if you are interested there are more involved rituals that you can perform. Here, I will explain the reasons that you may perform a ritual. I will also explain the steps that I take, and my reasons for following them.

Why Perform Ritual?

Rituals can serve many purposes for us. It could be a ritual to honor a holy day, or perhaps even a ritual to praise Abnoba for her continued guidance in your life. Maybe you want to make an offering and perform a spell. You could have a friend who is sick and in need of healing so you wish to call out Abnoba in Her capacity as a healer. The reasons are many. In this chapter I will outline a dedication ritual to Abnoba.

What Steps Must I Include in my Ritual?

I am moderately informal in the sense that I do not require myself to have an endless list of tools or take multiple steps as some traditions do. However, I do have a regular routine that I follow. If you feel inclined to take additional steps not included then please do so. If you feel something is repetitive and unnecessary then cut it out. You are free to alter these steps to meet your needs.

On the topic of ritual steps; I must note that nothing is wrong with elaborate steps. In fact, they can serve to really put your mind, body, and spirit where it needs to be to get your desired outcome. Just note that these steps are not required. I felt the need to include a template here because I know when I started devotional work that I wanted to know what others did in their practices.

It is important to keep in mind that dedicating yourself to any divine being is very serious and should only be done when you know you are ready. Some people even recommend honoring the deity for a year before deciding to make such a commitment. I feel that this is a good recommendation. It should also be noted that it is not necessary to dedicate yourself to any deity. As long as you treat the deity with respect you can continue to work with and honor them without dedication. Over the years I have honored a great number of deities, but I never dedicated myself to any one of them. Abnoba grew to be such an important part in my life. She was there for me at several critical moments. Before

I decided to write this book, I had gone through a very uncertain period. I felt as though She really lit my way out of the darkness. It was because of this that I did take the steps to dedicate myself to Her.

Making of Holy Water

Before beginning, there are a few simple pre-ritual tasks that I recommend. I start by making the holy water. I suggest leaving a jar outside to collect rainwater, or collecting it from a local stream. Alternatively, you can leave tap water out in the moonlight overnight to charge. You will then want to consecrate the water. This is a fairly simple step that you can prepare any time before the ritual. Simply hold the jar or bottle of water and say:

Abnoba,
You are the source of sacred waters.
You are the goddess of boundaries.
I ask that You bless this water
May You imbue it with power.

Personally, I try to keep a jar of holy water available at all times. I make it every so often under the full moon and then consecrate it the following morning.

Gather Ritual Items

After this, you will want to gather all of your supplies if they are not already at your altar. As previously discussed, each person will usually require different items for their altar, and that is fine. My suggestions for this ritual include everything mentioned earlier in the book: incense and holder, candle and offering dish plus a couple extras. I will list them below along with their purpose.

Holy Water

Water used in the ritual represents the sacred realm of Dumnos, the deep, or the Otherworld. That is why I feel it is important to use holy water instead of just pouring some water into the cauldron or offering dish. I feel it is particularly important to use in a dedicatory ritual. This goes without saying that water is sacred to Abnoba so it is a powerful representation of Her in the ritual.

Offering

As for the offering, a slice of fresh baked bread or cookies may be appropriate. Honey, maple syrup, fruits or nuts will all make great dedicatory offerings. Really anything I mentioned previously will suffice. Personally, I used bread for my dedication offering. However, feel free to be creative here as this is an important part of the ritual and a chance for you to really connect to Abnoba.

Please note that ritual is not exclusive to those who are financially advantaged. If you want to perform this ritual and do not have the funds for the suggested items then substitute them for whatever you can afford or find. I have been in situations where I would not have been able to afford the items listed but that did not stop me. It should not stop you either. Likewise, if there is something I did not list that you think is vitally important to ritual, please include it.

Preliminary Steps

The next step that I take is making sure my house is clean. This may sound strange, but I find this is very important to do before any ritual. As a goddess of the homestead, I see taking care of your home as a sacred act that I dedicate to Abnoba. Before inviting Her into your life, and your home, I find it best to start with a clean slate. There is no better way to do so than cleaning the house. Besides, you do not want to suddenly remember the pile of dishes collecting in the sink during the middle of a ritual.

After this you will cleanse yourself. Take your time and have a leisurely bath or shower. As previously noted, I make my own soap, something else that I find is sacred to Abnoba, and this is what I use to bathe. If you do not want to do that you can usually find a good bar of herbal soap at a local farmers market. If you take a bath, as opposed to a shower, use purifying herbs and place them in a muslin bag to soak in the water. This will help you to spiritually cleanse yourself. Utilize the time in the shower/bath to really unwind and ready your mind. Some people may suggest simply washing your hands and face. If you are just going in to make a prayer and offering then I think this will suffice. However, if you plan to perform a full ritual, I really recommend a shower or bath. You will be spiritually cleansing yourself again during the ritual with the holy water that was made earlier.

This should all go without saying that your altar, and altar room, should also be cleaned regularly. It needs to be cleaned both physically and spiritually just like you. This does not mean you cannot have a lot of stuff on your altar. You should just keep in mind that dust settles easily especially around multiple objects, and in my experience Abnoba is not a fan of that. Remember you are sharing this space with Her. Keeping your altar clean is a sign of reverence. To spiritually cleanse the room, I suggest burning incense or herbs, such as rosemary. This can be done at any time and as frequently as needed, but I really recommend doing so before every ritual.

If burning incense or herbs is an issue for you because of living arrangements, or smoke is a problem for you, there are alternatives. One such option is to take the bundle of herbs and dip them in some of your holy water and use that to sprinkle water around your altar room. Likewise, the incense that you will use can be replaced. In this case, simply use a fragrant herb such as lavender to stand in as a substitute. If a step calls for it, just waft the herbs around your work area instead of the incense.

The ritual format that I follow is very similar to the outline given in 'Ancient Fire' written by Segomâros Widugeni. Mine is a bit condensed for our purposes as we are only petitioning Abnoba in this ritual. You can use this template to set up other rituals you may wish to partake in later.

Purification

First is the ritual purification. This is where the holy water comes into play. Simply sprinkle a bit of the holy water on yourself and say:

I purify myself with this sacred water.
I purify myself so that I may enter this holy space as I come before the Gods.

Beginning

This step is actually divided into three parts. You begin with silence, then lighting of the sacred flame, followed by making the rampart. I will discuss each step in further detail below.

Silence

First, you want to center yourself in silence. This part of the ritual involves becoming mentally prepared. You need to be in the right headspace to continue. You do not want to be thinking about chores to be done, (after all this is why we made sure to clean the home first) or trying to remember something that you wanted to tell a friend. I suggest a few minutes of silence and meditation. Focus on your breathing. This will help to clear your mind of anything unnecessary to the ritual at hand.

Making Sacred Fire

This is the step where you will light the candle on your altar. The candle represents the spirit of the Gods during ritual. Again, if you cannot use a regular candle a battery powered one will suffice. As you light the candle say:

I light this sacred fire.
I light it to represent the Gods in this holy space.

Making the Rampart

In many traditions this step would be roughly equivalent to casting a circle. This step is taken to further designate the space as sacred, and to separate it from the profane. This step may not be necessary for everything that you do at your altar as your altar should be kept as a sacred space at all times. This step is fairly simple. You take the candle and move it in a circular motion above the altar moving from east to west. As you do this say:

I purify this holy space with this sacred flame.

Offering

Now is the time to make your offering. Place the offering on the offering dish, or pour the offering into a bowl depending on what you have chosen to offer. As you do this say:

I invoke Abnoba
Riganâ Milon
Dêuâ Antî
Dêuâ Allatês
Caruogenetâ
Mighty huntress of the wilds,
You protect the forest
I make this offering to you

Chant

Next, I will recite a chant as a part of my offering to Abnoba. In this chant I will present the terms of my service. Be sure that you are willing and able to remain committed to whatever it is that you promise. If you promise to offer freshly baked bread everyday keep in mind what a hard task that would be for anyone to do. Keep your promise in line with your capabilities. In the following I simply state that I will make an offering without specifics. I will usually offer incense or water, but occasionally I will offer freshly baked bread. This way I am not promising anything that I know I cannot deliver. I recite the following three times. Simply state:

Abnoba, in your service I will remain loyal to you.
Abnoba, in your service I promise a year of daily offerings to you.
Abnoba, in your service I promise to do good in your name.

Closing

This last part consists of saying thanks to Abnoba and putting out the sacred flame.

Thanks

This is where you will essentially say goodbye to Abnoba to close out the ritual. I simply say:

Abnoba,
Thank you for your presence today
Thank you for your gifts in my life
Thank you for your constant support
Abnoba, I praise you!

Covering the Sacred Fire

Now that you have thanked Abnoba you can extinguish your candle to signify that the ritual is officially closed.

If you are interested in performing other rituals you can still follow this general format. You can simply alter your chant request to something more appropriate. Additionally, the offering invocation can be changed to focus on a particular aspect of Abnoba that may be more suited to your intentions. With these changes you can invoke Abnoba in ritual for a variety of reasons. If you would like to learn more about Gaulish Polytheism and Gaulish ritual, I highly recommend 'Ancient Fire' by Segomâros Widugeni. This book not only goes into detail about ritual there is also great information on the Coligny Calendar and many other aspects of Gaulish Polytheism in general.

Conclusion

As you can see there really does not have to be a lot to a ritual. Again, feel free to add to this ritual as you see fit. What is most important is your intent. As long as you are focused and sincere then you should have no troubles. It is my hope that this ritual is easily accessible to all. As I said earlier, please make sure you are really ready before engaging in a dedication with any deity. It is a serious step that should not be taken lightly.

Conclusion

It is my fervent hope that you can now see the multitude of ways that Abnoba can enrich your life. Has She been calling out to you? Pay attention to the little things. When a deity contacts you, it is not always so obvious. Learn to see the signs and to intuit their meaning. Abnoba may not come up to you and smack you on the back of the head. In my experience She was much more subtle than that. We do not all get those mystical moments of realization, and that is okay.

We learned that the historical record is a fabulous way to learn about Abnoba. Unfortunately, where the record falls short, we must make up for it by reaching out to Her ourselves. One method of doing this is to compare and contrast other deities that may be similar to Abnoba. These cultures shared a similar origin at one point. It is possible that these 'sister' goddesses share certain roles.

Find aspects of Abnoba that call out to you specifically. Learn to work with these guises and find out how much She can truly benefit you when you reach out. Importantly, do not forget to celebrate Her! Everyone loves a good celebration and Abnoba is no different. There are multiple days throughout the year that can serve as holy days to Her.

As time goes by and your relationship seems to be getting stronger, dedicate a space to Abnoba. It is beneficial to Her by giving Abnoba a place of reverence. It provides you with a place to slip away from this mundane world and connect with Abnoba in the Otherworld. Use this sacred place to reach out through prayer, and learn to interact with Abnoba during meditation. These can be incredible tools to self-improvement.

Finally, say a year or more has gone by and you feel that this bond with Abnoba will only grow from this point, maybe it is time to dedicate yourself to Her. Learn to serve Her daily in your life and find out how much richer your life can become through this process. There are so many ways to establish a strong relationship with Abnoba. Her aspects are far from just a goddess of the hunt. She truly is a multifaceted deity. She longs to connect once again with Her descendants; that is, those who are truly wild at heart.

About the Author

Ryan McClain, also known as Tricûnos, has spent the last 25 years as a student and practitioner of various polytheistic traditions. He considers himself to be an animist with strong Gaulish Polytheistic leanings. As such, this greatly influences his spiritual path. He has honored many Gods and Goddesses throughout the years, but has grown particularly devoted to Abnoba over the last few years. He earned his degree in General Studies in 2010 for the purpose of gaining a broader base of knowledge. Since that time, he has indulged in independent study through various methods such as books, the internet, experimentation, meditation, prayer and any other means possible. Ryan resides in Terre Haute, Indiana where he lives with his husband, their three loveable dogs (Cali, Lulu, and Trixie), two slithering snakes (Ka & Persephone), a fiercely independent rabbit (Hazel), and one wacky bearded dragon (Thorn).

References

Athanassakis, A. N., Wolkow, B. M., & Orpheus. (2013). The Orphic hymns: Text, translation, and notes. Baltimore, Maryland: The John Hopkins University Press.

Barrett, D. (2010). How Can You Control Your Dreams? (Jordan Lite). Accessed on 06/23/2021 from https://www.scientificamerican.com/article/how-to-control-dreams/

Beck, N. (2009). *Goddesses in Celtic Religion Cult and Mythology*: A Comparative Study of Ancient Ireland, Britain and Gaul. Université Lumière Lyon. Accessed on 06/15/2021 from https://theses.univ-lyon2.fr/documents/lyon2/2009/beck_n/info

Bostock, J. Riley, H.T. & Pliny. (2018). *Pliny the Elder, Historia naturalis*. Project Gutenberg Accessed on 06/15/2021 from https://www.gutenberg.org/files/57493/57493-h/57493-h.htm#Footnote_2786

Catullus, G. V., Uzzi, J. D., & Thomson, J. (2015). The Poems of Catullus: An annotated translation.

Delamarre, X. (2003). Dictionnaire de la langue gauloise. Translated: Cassell, M. K. Paris, France: Errance.

Descoeudres, J. P. (1994) *Pompeii Revisited*: The Life and Death of a Roman Town. Sydney: Meditarch. Accessed on 06/16/2021 from http://www.u.arizona.edu/~afutrell/404b/web%20rdgs/tour%20pomp/larartour.htm

Gimbutas, M. (1999). *The Living Goddesses*. Berkley: University of California Press.

Gingras B, Pohler G, Fitch W.T. (2014). *Exploring Shamanic Journeying*: Repetitive Drumming with Shamanic Instructions Induces Specific Subjective Experiences but No Larger Cortisol Decrease than Instrumental Meditation Music. PLoS ONE 9(7): e102103. https://doi.org/10.1371/journal.pone.0102103

Green, M. (1992). *Animals in Celtic Myth and Life*. New York, NY: Routledge.

Grieshaber, F. (n.d.). Inscriptions: Simple Search - Epigraphic Database Heidelberg. https://edh-www.adw.uni-heidelberg. de/inschrift/suche?qs=abnoba

Griffith, R. T. H. (1896). *The Rig Veda*. Accessed on 6/18/2021 from https://www.sacred-texts.com/hin/rigveda/index.htm

Hellenion. (N.D.). *Artemis*, Hellenic Practice and Connecting with the Goddess. Accessed on 06/25/2021 from https:// www.hellenion.org/essays-on-hellenic-polytheism/artemis-hellenic-practice-and-connecting-with-the-goddess/

Hesiod, & Evelyn-White, H. G. (1920). *Hesiod, the Homeric hymns and Homerica*. New York: Putnam

Horn, H. (2014). *Abnoba*: A Summary of Old and New Research. Accessed on 06/15/2021 from https://www.researchgate.net/ publication/337448533_Abnoba_Eine_Zusammenfassung_ alter_und_neuer_Forschungserkenntnisse

Nouiogalatis. (2019). *Cingo Ammanes* (Calendar). Accessed on 06/25/2021 from https://nouiogalatis.org/2019/12/11/ sequanni-coligny-calendar/

Novaroma, Editors of. (2009). *Nemoralia*. Accessed on 06/20/2021 from http://www.novaroma.org/nr/Nemoralia

Price, S., Kearns, E. (Eds.). (2003). *The Oxford Dictionary of Classical Myth and Religion*. New York: Oxford University Press Inc.

Ritchie, H., Roser, M. (2021). *Forests and Deforestation*. Published online at OurWorldInData.org. Retrieved from: https:// ourworldindata.org/forests-and-deforestation on 07/03/2021

Statius, P. P., & Mozley, J. H. (1928). Statius, Thebaid. Cambridge: Harvard University Press. Accessed on 06/22/2021 from https://www.theoi.com/Text/StatiusThebaid4.html

Tacitus, C. (2013). *The Germany and the Agricola of Tacitus*. Project Gutenberg. Accessed on 06/15/2021 from https://www. gutenberg.org/files/7524/7524-h/7524-h.htm

Widugeni, Segomaros. (2018). *Ancient Fire*. Amelia, Ohio: ADF

Publishing.

Li Q. (2010). *Effect of forest bathing trips on human immune function.* Environmental health and preventive medicine, 15(1), 9–17. https://doi.org/10.1007/s12199-008-0068-3

Coligny Calendar Application by Canabirix Sapouaððion https://www.coligny-app.com/

MOON
BOOKS

PAGANISM & SHAMANISM

What is Paganism? A religion, a spirituality, an alternative
belief system, nature worship? You can find support for all these
definitions (and many more) in dictionaries, encyclopaedias, and
text books of religion, but subscribe to any one and the truth will
evade you. Above all Paganism is a creative pursuit, an encounter
with reality, an exploration of meaning and an expression of the
soul. Druids, Heathens, Wiccans and others, all contribute their
insights and literary riches to the Pagan tradition. Moon Books
invites you to begin or to deepen your own encounter, right here,
right now.

If you have enjoyed this book, why not tell other readers by
posting a review on your preferred book site.

Recent bestsellers from Moon Books are:

Journey to the Dark Goddess
How to Return to Your Soul
Jane Meredith
Discover the powerful secrets of the Dark Goddess and
transform your depression, grief and pain into healing
and integration.
Paperback: 978-1-84694-677-6 ebook: 978-1-78099-223-5

Shamanic Reiki
Expanded Ways of Working with Universal Life Force Energy
Llyn Roberts, Robert Levy
Shamanism and Reiki are each powerful ways of healing; together,
their power multiplies. *Shamanic Reiki* introduces techniques to
help healers and Reiki practitioners tap ancient healing wisdom.
Paperback: 978-1-84694-037-8 ebook: 978-1-84694-650-9

Pagan Portals – The Awen Alone
Walking the Path of the Solitary Druid
Joanna van der Hoeven
An introductory guide for the solitary Druid, *The Awen Alone* will
accompany you as you explore, and seek out your own place
within the natural world.
Paperback: 978-1-78279-547-6 ebook: 978-1-78279-546-9

A Kitchen Witch's World of Magical Herbs & Plants
Rachel Patterson
A journey into the magical world of herbs and plants, filled with
magical uses, folklore, history and practical magic. By popular
writer, blogger and kitchen witch, Tansy Firedragon.
Paperback: 978-1-78279-621-3 ebook: 978-1-78279-620-6

Medicine for the Soul
The Complete Book of Shamanic Healing
Ross Heaven
All you will ever need to know about shamanic healing and how to become your own shaman...
Paperback: 978-1-78099-419-2 ebook: 978-1-78099-420-8

Shaman Pathways – The Druid Shaman
Exploring the Celtic Otherworld
Danu Forest
A practical guide to Celtic shamanism with exercises and techniques as well as traditional lore for exploring the Celtic Otherworld.
Paperback: 978-1-78099-615-8 ebook: 978-1-78099-616-5

Traditional Witchcraft for the Woods and Forests
A Witch's Guide to the Woodland with Guided Meditations and Pathworking
Mélusine Draco
A Witch's guide to walking alone in the woods, with guided meditations and pathworking.
Paperback: 978-1-84694-803-9 ebook: 978-1-84694-804-6

Wild Earth, Wild Soul
A Manual for an Ecstatic Culture
Bill Pfeiffer
Imagine a nature-based culture so alive and so connected, spreading like wildfire. This book is the first flame...
Paperback: 978-1-78099-187-0 ebook: 978-1-78099-188-7

Naming the Goddess
Trevor Greenfield
Naming the Goddess is written by over eighty adherents and
scholars of Goddess and Goddess Spirituality.
Paperback: 978-1-78279-476-9 ebook: 978-1-78279-475-2

Shapeshifting into Higher Consciousness
Heal and Transform Yourself and Our World with Ancient
Shamanic and Modern Methods
Llyn Roberts
Ancient and modern methods that you can use every day to
transform yourself and make a positive difference in the world.
Paperback: 978-1-84694-843-5 ebook: 978-1-84694-844-2

Readers of ebooks can buy or view any of these bestsellers by
clicking on the live link in the title. Most titles are published in
paperback and as an ebook. Paperbacks are available in traditional
bookshops. Both print and ebook formats are available online.

Find more titles and sign up to our readers' newsletter at
http://www.johnhuntpublishing.com/paganism
Follow us on Facebook at https://www.facebook.com/MoonBooks
and Twitter at https://twitter.com/MoonBooksJHP